KICK ASS IN COLLEGE

It's more than a guide to doing well in college… It's a guide through life.

> René Mario Scherr
> Graduate
> Stanford University

Solid, "real world" advice… for students seeking to use their degree as a springboard to an exciting career.

> Barbara Eureste, Director
> Liberal Arts Career Placement Center
> University of Texas at Austin

The first "How to Succeed in College" book that didn't give me a pounding headache. Great tips, Gunnar! You rock!

> Mike Scott
> Freshman
> UCLA

Gunnar's advice will save students a lot of heartache. Kick Ass in College is a triumph of frankness, rewarding its readers with a bracing splash of reality and invaluable coaching for college.

> Dr. John Barberet
> Professor
> University of Central Florida

Since using your study methods and career advice in law school I have been "kicking ass" in a big way. It took seeing the real world and experiencing paycheck-to-paycheck life (as a police officer) for me to realize how important it is to take full advantage of my educational opportunities. My academic confidence has made a huge difference in how I carry myself during job interviews.... Good job, Mr. Fox! You're helping a lot of people achieve their dreams.

Bryan Rose
First-Year Law Student
St. Mary's University Law School

This book has more useful content than all of the other college prep books on the market combined. Even before I stepped into my first college classroom I was using Gunnar's hints and ideas to prepare myself to succeed.... If I could give one piece of advice to college students and high school seniors it would be "Buy this book."

Randall Andrews
Freshman
Iowa State University

ABOUT THE AUTHOR

"Gen Y and Z – look out. The force of nature known as Gunnar Fox is here to kick your ass into academic shape."

College success guides won't help students if they don't read them. But they'll definitely read this one! Sure, *Kick Ass in College* is irreverent and laugh-out-loud funny. But author Gunnar Fox is out for more than just the sound of his readers' laughter: he wants their full attention and commitment to his kick-ass study techniques and life strategies.

Gunnar has no time for pussyfooting around the difficult issues students face in college – or in the highly competitive job market that awaits them. This is a high-octane, no-fluff guide to success that one university professor describes as "…a triumph of frankness that rewards its readers with a bracing splash of reality and invaluable coaching for college."

The experience of reading *Kick Ass in College* is much like having a conversation–one that will echo in students' minds throughout college and beyond. In addition to providing his step-by-step blueprint for classroom success, Gunnar tackles relationships, substance abuse, and a host of other real-world issues, all with his trademark combination of raucous humor and bone-chilling candor.

Gunnar's perspective is that of a person young enough to have college in his rear-view mirror–but experienced enough to have enjoyed success in the professional world. Gunnar graduated with honors from a host of fancy schools including Andover and Stanford Law School. When he isn't teaching his thrill-a-minute *Kick Ass in College*™ Seminars, Gunnar practices international and high-tech law, runs a real estate investment business and publishing company, and writes all sorts of things. He divides his time between Dallas, Texas and Bangkok, Thailand.

Also from KickAssMedia

The *Kick Ass in College* Audiobook on CD

Coming soon from KickAssMedia

Kick Ass at Work
The *Kick Ass at Work* Audiobook on CD

Coming soon from Instinct Learning

The Frontline Spanish Course for Law Enforcement
The Frontline Spanish Course for EMS Technicians

**Please visit www.kickasscampus.com
for more great products.**

A Guerrilla Guide
to College Success

GUNNAR FOX

Gunnar Fox, Your Personal Success Coach
Teaches You How to Win in College ... and Beyond

DALLAS, TEXAS • BANGKOK, THAILAND

Published in the United States by KickAssMedia, Publisher Loftus J. Carlson III, 12358 Coit Road, PMB #317, Dallas, Texas 75251-2308. **1-877-MY-COOL-BOOK** (1-877-692-6652). First edition. KickAssMedia is a division of Nana Plaza, LLC, Dallas, Texas and Bangkok, Thailand.

To order additional copies visit **www.kickassmedia.com**. KickAssMedia and Instinct Learning products are available at special quantity discounts for bulk purchases to be used for sales promotions, premiums, fund-raising or educational use. Special books or book excerpts can also be created to fit specific needs. For details, contact publisher@kickassmedia.com.

Cover design, illustrations: Scott Reed
www.websbestdesigns.com, www.websbestcomics.com
Edited by Hector Calderon
Author photos by Elizabeth Lavin

To collect your FREE gift worth $49.95 send an email to:
gift@kickassincollege.com

Publisher's Cataloging-in-Publication Data
Second Printing, 2005
Fox, Gunnar.
Gunnar Fox's Kick ass in college : a guerrilla guide to college success / Gunnar Fox. 1st ed. -- Dallas, Texas : KickAssMedia, 2004.
p. ; cm.
Includes bibliographical references and index.
ISBN: 0976292823
1. Student adjustment--United States. 2. College environment--United States. 3. Academic achievement--United States. 4. College attendance--United States. 5. College students--United States--Conduct of life. I. Title. II. Kick ass in college.
LB1139.S88 F69 2004
378.1/98/0973--dc22 0501   2004116298

To my parents, Harold and Sara, for never letting me lose sight of the value of a good education – something no one can ever take away from you.

Contents

There are times in life when a handful of critical information makes all the difference in the world. —**G.F.**

Preface

O kay, so you're into college. Now it's time for you to make a highly conscious decision: *I will kick ass in college.*

Say it.

Feels good, huh?

By the way, I'm not just talking about racking up good grades, though that's at the heart of this plan. I'm also talking about using the college experience as a launch pad to success in life–real life, not just life in a classroom.

Have you ever had a conversation that just blew your mind? Has someone ever opened doors for you with just a few words? I know it can happen because it's happened to me. I want this to be one of those conversations.

So let's start talking.

Acknowledgements

KICK ASS in COLLEGE could not have been possible without the wealth of inspiration I received from many of my own instructors over the years, notably Ada Fan and Lou Bernieri at Phillips Academy, Andover; Robert Kane and the late, truly great Chad Oliver of the Plan II Honors Program of the University of Texas at Austin; and Barbara Babcock and Robert Rabin of Stanford Law School.

I am also proud to thank my hundreds of students for the privilege of working with them to refine my study and life strategies.

My deep appreciation goes out to the generous "Kick Ass Success Team" – surely the most accomplished cadre of young professionals ever assembled – for the wisdom they have shared in the vignettes that so enrich the book. The quasi-anonymous team included: Rich Andrews, Ron Antush, Roy Atwood, Matt Berenson, Jay Bhattacharya, McKay Cunningham, Bob DeCarli, Douglas Coyle, Ross Garsson, Debbie Eberts, Jay Johnson, Kay Kennedy, Kristina Kennedy, Lara Kennedy, Congressman Patrick Kennedy, Britt Latham, Margaret Lyle, Mike MacDougal, Leane Medford, Chris Mittleman, Phil Mittleman, Mark Niermann, Mike Newton, Jason Owsley, Michael Pratt, Simon Rajwani, Mark Reiter, René Mario Scherr, Peter Schroeder, John Ward, Barry Williams and Debbie Whalen.

My agents at Dupree Miller Associates, Michael Broussard and Jan Miller, deserve special mention for their tireless efforts to promote the book. I am honored to be among your clients.

Another humbling honor I've received is the chance to work with the legendary Alan Aldridge, who designed our amazing "Kick Ass" logo. And the incandescently talented Scott Reed's illustrations and other design work on this and other projects have been truly inspired. Thank you both.

Lastly, I would be egregiously remiss (and likely homeless) if I did not offer a very special thanks to my brilliant girlfriend Kristina Kennedy for her enormous patience, astute counsel and unwavering support as I tackled this undertaking.

GUNNAR FOX
Dallas, 2005

A Note to Students

This book isn't any longer than it needs to be so I'd appreciate it if you'd read the whole thing.

GUNNAR FOX
Dallas, 2005

A Note to Parents

My philosophy for students is embarrassingly simple: If you really want to have a blast in college, do well in college.

Kick Ass in College focuses on two areas: (1) developing the proper mindset for college, and (2) practical survival skills for any student leaving home for the first time. While I primarily reference the freshman year of college, virtually any student will benefit from reading this book.

My overriding goal is to teach students a few fundamental principles without boring the pants off of them. Accordingly, I don't overload them with reams of information. In my experience, peppy and pithy work a lot better than ponderous and professorial.

As you look at the other college manuals on the shelf ask yourself, "Would Junior really want to slog through this?" Because if they don't read it, it won't help them. Frankly, it's hard to imagine anything more mind-numbingly boring to a kid than being asked to study a book *that is itself about studying*. As interesting, witty and illuminating as this book is, we'll be lucky if it doesn't end up in the rectangular file after a couple of chapters.

In an attempt to avoid that outcome, I've actually written something entertaining, that students can turn to again and again for encouragement, inspiration and focus. It is my strong belief that the wisdom in this book will continue to guide students well after college, as they make their way in the professional world.

So here's the plan: we're going to keep things brief but substantive. And I'm going to tell things from my perspective – that of somebody young enough to still have college in my rear-view mirror but old enough to have demonstrated repeatedly and beyond any doubt that my strategies work.*

And so, esteemed parents, feel free to join us on this 200-plus page thrill ride back to college. In the words of noted philosopher, Fat Albert, "If you're not careful, you may learn something."

GUNNAR FOX
Dallas, 2005

---

* What, exactly, are my credentials? A fair question. After graduating from fancy-pants prep school at Andover I matriculated to the highly competitive Plan II Honors Program at the University of Texas at Austin. There I was elected President of the Student Council for my 10,000-member college and named Dean's Distinguished Graduate. Fresh out of college, I accepted a position as a Student Development Specialist for the University, developing a study program for so-called "at-risk" students that decreased the attrition rate among this group by a whopping 65 percent. From there it was on to Stanford Law School, where I served as an editor of the Law Review and built a sterling transcript that landed me a plum job at the largest law firm in the country. These days, aside from a successful career in high-tech and international law, I run a profitable real estate business and a thriving publishing company. Did I mention I am now working on my fourth language? Blah blah blah, yada yada yada...What I'm really trying to say is, don't worry–I've got plenty of "street cred" to go with my loads of "academic cred" so they're in good hands. Unlike some egghead study geek who rarely ventures beyond the safe confines of academia, I will make sure that my students are truly ready for the tough job market that awaits. When I'm done with them, they'll be school-smart–*and* street-smart.

Whether you realize it or not, whether you intend it or not, whether you like it or not—the first thing that affects anything you do is your mindset. — **G.F.**

Chapter I

College: "Get Over It"

Why I Bothered To Write This

When I was an academic advisor at the University of Texas at Austin, I read almost every "How to Succeed in College" book available. A few of them were pretty good. I guess they just weren't good enough, because here we are.

Most traditional college manuals give you basically the same information: "College is much harder than high school, so study hard, keep your pencils sharpened and your nose clean." Unfortunately, somebody with a Ph.D. in education might take several hundred pages to say this.

Well, it's true that college is generally more challenging than high school. It also stands to reason that hard work and good study skills are helpful in achieving success in college. But do you feel ready to **kick ass** in college based on that information? I doubt it.

Again, that's why we're here. Some books make you eat your way through the whole box of cereal before you get the prize at the bottom. I've tried to make this one more like a box of prizes.

I'm not suggesting that this guide will answer all of your questions about college life. But I can promise you that we'll cover a lot of real-world information that tends to get ignored... plus some other incredibly useful stuff you probably weren't expecting to find here.

Ready to kick ass?

In the course of our time together you will encounter the happy little **foot-kicking-ass symbol** above, along with quotes from former students with something to say about the topic at hand. These anonymous little insights and vignettes have only one thing in common: they all came from people who are exceptionally successful today. (I felt it was so important to gather these pearls of wisdom that I even asked successful people I don't even particularly like to contribute. So I hope you appreciate it.) — **G.F.**

Ooooh ... "College"

irst of all, let's get this college thing into perspective. Some of you are *waaay* too impressed by the place you are going to spend the next four years or so. If you experience fear, awe or confusion when you think about attending College, prepare to ditch all of that.

Hey, it's normal to feel a little intimidated by your majestic new home away from home, with its stately buildings and endless streams of brilliant students. But it is imperative that you make a deliberate effort to **get over it.**

Do not allow any aspect of your college–whether it pertains to academics, administration, or student organizations–to retain its mystique for very long. I'm not telling you to adopt an attitude of blasé sophistication. No one would be able to stand you. **I'm saying you must aggressively pursue information about how your school functions from the first day of classes.**

Think of yourself as a predator (like a shark or a mongoose or something) alertly and confidently seeking out its prey. If something looks interesting as you walk through campus, take a minute to kill and eat it (so to speak). Read a kiosk. Dart in a cool building. Search the school website. Crawl through the underbrush and track a squirrel.

If you operate in this predatory mindset, you will root out countless resources and opportunities. What you find may not all be relevant now but information has a way of making itself useful sooner or later. And this practice will give you a useful bird's-eye perspective on how your school works.

Our underlying goal is to find ways for you to avoid freshman potholes. You hit potholes when you don't look far enough down the road, or when you haven't learned how to steer around unpleasant surprises. But I'll show you how to anticipate the future and respond nimbly when it arrives. A lot of people regard it as tradition that freshmen must endure all sorts of trials, tribulations and humiliations during their first year at school. I think we can agree that you'll want to break with that tradition.

My first year of college was a joke. My roommates and I basically acted like wild animals that had broken free from their cages. Being away from home was incredibly intoxicating. People like to say, "I wouldn't change a thing" about my college experience. Not me. I found myself in a lot of unpleasant situations, academic and otherwise. I would have had a lot more fun had I tried to strike a little better balance. On the one hand, you could say "it's all just part of growing up." But I spent the next five years making up for that first lost year, right up until the end. —**M.J.**

It's simple, really. While others have their blinders on you will be improving the quality of your information....

Information gives you *Options*.
When you have options you have *Freedom of Choice*.
And when you have freedom of choice you take *Control*.
If there is one overriding theme in the advice that follows it is **"Take Control!"**

Much of the pressure new students face is a direct result of not being in control. They fail to seek academic help, or neglect their class syllabus deadlines. They might miss important orientation sessions, or fail to address a destructive roommate situation.

There are help and answers for those who seek them. There are myriad academic counselors, peer advisors, faculty and staff with whom you can speak. There are numerous information booklets and new student guides you can read. Sadly, some freshmen expect to be lovingly spoon-fed by Professor Mommy. Well, unless your mom teaches Cultural Anthropology it ain't gonna happen.

Professor Mommy! Waaaaah!

Most colleges and universities, especially the larger ones, give you a solid introduction to the real world. When you leave college and enter the job market, no one is going to stop you on the sidewalk and ask if they can help you file your taxes. Similarly, academic counselors will rarely pull you aside because they suspect you might need a German tutor.

So to reiterate, this is how I think you should play the Game of College:

You must not allow yourself to be ruled by circumstances, time constraints, ignorance – or unproductive relationships with negative people who are not going to get you a job or pay your bills when you get out of college.

The day you step on campus, take control of your circumstances and take action to change whatever you must.

Stay tuned for more on this.

Job Description

If you ask a group of average college students why they are attending college, many will say "to get a job." In a very important sense, they are mistaken. **They already have a job.**

College is a job. Think of it as a four-year entry-level position into adulthood. As with any job, you must put in a certain number of hours a day. You were hired to do your job the day you were accepted. The longer you avoid this potentially terrifying reality, the less successful you will be.

This warning may fall on deaf ears among those of you who were lucky enough to have been spoiled by your parents. You may still be under the impression that your purpose in life is "to please mom and dad so they'll get off my back and keep making the payments on my new Jetta." But you're in the Big Leagues now. Unless your folks are eager to share their retirement savings with you, you will need to take drastic measures to preserve your lifestyle.

For many of you, the college years can be pretty lean times. If nothing else inspires you to action, ponder the idea of living on Ramen noodles, Mac n' Cheese and Hot Pockets for the rest of your life. *Ick.*

Your job as a college student entails various responsibilities, some of which should be fairly obvious. Stay with me as I quickly summarize them:

- Attending class–**without fail**. (There is no substitute whatsoever for classroom learning.)

- Performing homework for your classes–**nightly**. (Cramming is no substitute for steady learning over the course of a semester.)

- Turning in assignments and essays **on time**.(College deadlines are serious business.)

- Aggressively seeking positions of responsibility and leadership in **extracurricular organizations**. (Pursuing these opportunities while managing classwork is a juggling act that you must master in order to build a superior resume.)

- Funding your **college tuition, room & board**. (This could mean obtaining financial aid assistance and – if truly necessary – performing a work-study or other income-generating job to support yourself.)

You will soon notice that many of your fellow students are treating college like an extended Club Med® vacation. It's unwise to follow their lead. Don't be fooled into believing that bizarre behavior and rash acts of irresponsibility will benefit you, or them, in any way. "Animal House" was a cool movie – but the jerk throwing up off of the balcony of your dorm is no John Belushi.

Treating college like an extended vacation?

You are a professional student, and you need to focus on going to work and getting "paid" (*i.e.*, making the grade). If your focus is elsewhere, you won't hit your goals and you'll wind up as the employee of someone who *did* focus.

Should have gotten your sh*t together.

Look At The Big Picture

If you are poised for success and armed with the knowledge of what to expect, the result will be confidence. That confidence, in turn, will produce focus and vision. As a first-year student, you will have more knowledge of how to play the college game than do many seniors.

Some of what I will tell you in this guide may sound mercenary. Some of it is kind of mercenary. All of it will help you. For the more squeamish among you, just remember three things:

1. I will never advise you to do anything dishonest or unreasonably selfish. The surest way to achieve success in college is by making the greatest possible contribution to the life of the institution. Yet in order to do this, you must make a name for yourself, developing your reputation and your expertise as a student and, over time, as a student leader. Consequently, your achievements will naturally be more impressive than those of many of your peers. If this makes you feel uncomfortable or guilty, stop reading now.

2. The college or university you will attend is a fine institution with long-heralded traditions. But notably, it is also a business. It may be the home of a great many virtuous and learned people whom you will be privileged to meet, but it is a business just the same. Though you are a student who has come to receive and create knowledge, you are also a client who has come to receive a service, and ultimately, a degree. *Without you, there would be no need for the institution.*

3. Sharp, articulate, accomplished graduates are much valued by colleges and universities. Nobody wants to graduate a schmo. Upon graduation, you will be a "product" of the institution. You may one day be called upon to represent your alma mater as a recipient of its excellent educational preparation. Thus, college officials want you to avail yourself of every opportunity for leadership and achievement possible. Every year they are on the lookout for students who distinguish themselves. One day, you may be a famous political, business or literary figure who will bring much prestige to your campus. In short, your success in college will benefit *everyone,* so a lot of people are rooting for you.

College will be an exhilarating, consciousness-raising experience. You will enjoy the lectures of fascinating professors who will challenge and excite you. Indeed, it may be the most remarkable period of intellectual growth you will ever experience.

But college is also a building block, simple as that. Your degree is a steppingstone over the tumultuous river of adolescence into the next phase of maturity. Therefore, you must assure that you get something very valuable out of the college experience–something roughly equivalent in value to the thousands of dollars it will cost you to attend: You must obtain a powerful degree and a resume that will propel you to the next level of your career.

What's College Got To Do With It?

T he more you can get out of college, the better prepared you will be to handle career challenges down the line. Seems crazy but lots of students take the attitude that college is somehow irrelevant to the "real world." Granted, maybe it *seems* like a literature course on Chaucerian Courtly Love won't be of much use in tackling that investment banking job after graduation. But let's look more closely at this conclusion. Check out all the ways this class *will* help you if you put your heart in it:

- You'll hone your skills in reading and writing about complex, unfamiliar topics (as you will be called upon to do in any white-collar job);

- You'll learn to express yourself and communicate a point of view in front of a group of critical thinkers (your fellow students) in a professional setting (a classroom);

- You'll learn how to allocate your resources to meet key deadlines (get used to it);

- You'll learn how to deal effectively with your supervisor (your professor);

- You'll obtain that cocktail-party polish necessary to compete in the sophisticated Wall Street shark tank you may be swimming in one day (A well-rounded education is a potent tool for schmoozing clients).

Now you tell me, how is that any different from what you'll be doing in a business suit in a fancy office a few years from now? If you're looking for the "real world" of your future, look no further: *you're in it, baby.* Coast in college and it may stunt your career. Perform in college and you'll shine like a diamond.

Chapter I

College: "Get Over It"

Key Points

1. Do not allow any aspect of college life to remain a mystery. Root out resources and opportunities to avoid freshman potholes.

2. Options = Freedom of Choice = Control

3. College is a job.

4. Believe it or not, you are developing the same basic skill set in college that you will rely upon daily in your future profession.

College is the place you go to become a human being you would want to meet and an employee you would want to hire. —**G.F.**

Chapter II

Cutting Through The Crap: Why People Are Willing To Spend Thousands To Earn A College Degree

"The Two Americas"

Just because a politician running for office says something doesn't always make it a lie: Yes, there really are "two Americas."[1] There's the educated, mostly prosperous America... and the under-educated, often struggling America.

A government study in 1995 and determined that the average college graduate makes **74 percent more** than somebody with only a high school diploma. And this earnings gap is widening (in 1974 there was only a 38 percent difference). You are reading this book because you are committed to being on the right side of this grim divide. Good for you.

Have Fun, Grow And Keep Your Eyes On That Damn Piece Of Paper

If you were to go to college for four years and take one unit short of what you need to get your degree, you would probably learn a great deal. You might learn how to analyze a complex business deal or acquire a scholarly knowledge of world affairs. Perhaps you would learn to design a steel bridge or program a powerful database. But you would *not* receive your degree, the specific credential you are there to earn.

Our society is extremely "credential-oriented." People are highly focused on whether you have a degree or a title or some other "credential" to make you "cred-ible." Cynics might say that whether you have actual knowledge or skill is less important than whether you have a nice piece of paper to hang on your wall. But like it or not, that is your present-day reality. **No matter what anybody tells you, failing to obtain your degree is not an option.**

You will never, never *ever* regret formally completing your education. Your degree will continue to be a symbol of achievement and an asset throughout your life whether you remain in one profession or transition throughout several careers. People who do not obtain their degrees (even highly successful people) tend to regret it.

Nevertheless, some still try to minimize the importance of earning a degree. They cite a number of famous entrepreneurs in the Fortune 500 and point out that *they* never graduated from college. That's like saying the less you know about building a mousetrap, the better your mousetrap will be. Whether or not you learn exactly how to build a mousetrap, make sure you leave college with your degree.

In theory, anybody can win the lottery and stumble into a fabulous career without ever obtaining a formal education. But not very many people do. Again, if you look at it simply in terms of salary potential, those with college degrees earn, on average, well over half a million dollars more over their lifetimes than those who do not. Whether you place a high priority on money, you have to admit — there are a lot of worse things you could have in your pocket. (Like a week-old meatball sub or some pissed-off hornets.)

Employers view academic achievement in the form of a degree as the best indicator of your future success. You must prepare to be judged on these terms. Do I think a fancy degree and good grades are always the best indicator of ability or intelligence? No. There are a lot more people with fantastic potential who don't have educational opportunities than there are hotshots lucky enough to be in college. But when an employer asks you to disclose your G.P.A. and you stink up the joint what do you expect them to do? They have their own job to protect! Help them out and give them a G.P.A. they can work with. Remember: **Nobody ever got fired for hiring an excellent student.**

Don't stink up the joint.

In The End, Everybody Has The Same Job

If you think about it, what do good grades really say about a person? Well, they might say you are "smart." But as you'll read later, most anybody has the level of intelligence required to succeed in college.

Truth is, what employers are actually looking for is evidence that you could fit into their organization and conform to their system of doing things. (There'll be time to innovate and break the rules later – after you've paid some dues and mastered their existing system.)

It so happens that college is also a system. It is a system of rules, regulations, requirements and expectations. The degree, along with your strong G.P.A. and impressive extracurricular record, tells prospective employers or graduate schools that you have been able to conform to and master a system. This, in turn, says you can follow directions. It says that you know how to deal with all kinds of people and show respect when it is due. In other words, they can feel fairly confident that you're not a complete A-hole.

If there's one thing I've learned in the professional world it's that everybody has basically the same job: to eliminate problems for somebody else. For example, if you are a junior engineer working on part of a car's brake system your job is to solve problems for the head engineer in charge of the whole car. And it's her job to solve problems for the business manager in charge of the whole car division. And so on and so on, all the way up to the CEO who is responsible to the Board of Directors who are ultimately responsible to the individual shareholders (who can collectively fire everybody).

At every level of the chain there has to be a reliable, competent person willing to take responsibility for problems or the whole thing breaks down.

If you needed to hire somebody to solve problems for you, what kind of person would it be? That, my friends, is exactly the kind of person you want to think about becoming.

Graduate On Time

Commit to learning the rules of the credential game. For starters, that means simply keeping track of the number of credits required to graduate so you stay on schedule. No matter what major you choose, sit down with an academic advisor and figure out:

(a) how many credits you need, and

(b) which specific classes you'll need to take to get your degree (or –if you are temporarily "undeclared"–to at least stay on track until you select a major).

Be careful: your school will usually have a number of math and science requirements, for example, that may not seem to have much to do with majoring in Art History. But failure to comply could derail your exit strategy from college for months or longer.

Document these requirements, including the proper number of credits you need annually. Post this information on your bulletin board and reference it–often. I can't tell you how many times students screw this up by selecting the wrong classes and then finding out that they can't graduate on time.

As a general matter, you should meet with your academic advisor at least once a semester, whether you perceive that you need to or not. First, this will help avoid unexpected surprises. Second, this will allow you to forge a connection with your particular advisor (try to see the same one every time if the relationship is working).

Easy Credits: Plucking The Low-Hanging Fruit

By the way, remember to inquire whether you qualify to obtain "free" credits by virtue of Achievement Tests, Advanced Placement Exams, College Level Examinations or through your school's own standardized testing programs. Students often miss the chance to rack up a slew of credit hours, or even credits that may count toward your G.P.A. as A's, through these processes. Recognize also that your own language skills–Chinese, Spanish, whatever–may earn you free credits if you can score well enough on standardized tests. And it doesn't matter a bit whether you've ever even taken an actual class in that language or not!

If you are so inclined, you can potentially shave a year or more off of your college career and save several thousand dollars in tuition through taking College Level Examinations by first enrolling in relatively easy and quick College Level Exam Preparation ("CLEP") mini-courses. For more information on CLEP testing, visit **www. kickasscampus.com**.

Surprisingly, relatively few students are aware of these options. I happen to believe most colleges don't go out of their way to suggest that you take advantage of CLEP opportunities to keep students in school for the traditional four years. While I am not necessarily a fan of blasting through college in two or three years these tactics can afford you a nice G.P.A. buffer. Personally, I would rather graduate with a 3.7 G.P.A. in four years than with a 3.0 in three years. Think about it …. Which will serve you better, an outstanding job opportunity (or admission to an elite graduate school)–or a few thousand bucks saved by skipping out of a semester or two of college? Savvy students simply use CLEP testing as a way to stockpile credits and avoid lousy requirements.

Use Your Local Community College To Boost Your G.P.A.

Look, I believe that we need to learn to find pleasure and satisfaction in tasks we don't necessarily want to perform in order to be successful. But that doesn't mean you can't occasionally water down an unpleasant obligation if you can do so without negative consequences.

Let's say you plan to get a degree in marketing but you know you still have to fulfill a science requirement by taking physics or chemistry. If you aren't especially jazzed about science it will be tough to ace the class. This might be a golden opportunity for you to fulfill this requirement at community college – where the class may be somewhat less intense. If you do well enough, you'll probably get your credit on something akin to a pass/fail basis (see below), since the grade itself may not transfer. Even so, your grade will probably need to be at least a "B" in the class to be eligible for credit.

The key is to make sure you verify whether the conditions required for you to fulfill the requirement at your four-year college can be met through a community college course. Politely request to speak with a senior administrator (not a peer advisor) from your college to make certain the information you receive is correct, and get their advice in writing. Again, never assume information received from the community college itself is necessarily accurate. Only trust *your* college or university on such key matters.

When putting your curriculum together, don't feel that you need to take all "serious" classes. Have some fun. For instance, my university offered a class called the "History of Rock n' Roll." This was a two-semester class, because, as we all know, a professor can't teach something as complex as the history of rock n' roll in just one semester. There's a lot to cover, what with Sammy Hagar and Slash. The professor declared that tests were not only open book, but "open mind." In other words, long as you could come up with some general opinions about music to scribble into your essay booklet, you'd ace the test. Before the university administration "revised" the class, it was a guaranteed "A." The lesson: there are ways to obtain get an easy "A" without killing yourself. Seek and you shall find. —**N.S.**

GOOD MORNING, PROFESSOR COHEN'S 2 O'CLOCK CLASS!!!
ARE YOU READY TO ROCK???

Pass/Fail Your Way Over G.P.A. Speedbumps

There will be a multitude of G.P.A.-boosting strategies in future chapters. But while we're on the general topic of accumulating the necessary credits to obtain your degree let's discuss the tactic of taking selected classes on a pass/fail or credit/no-credit basis. This generally means you get credit so long as you earn a "C." Equally important, the actual grade you make in a pass/fail class, for better or worse–be it an "A," "B," or "C"–does *not* get factored into your G.P.A. This can be a *huge* benefit.

Most of the time, I urge students to try to find the beauty in each subject they study, to muster all the enthusiasm they can so that they can joyfully suck the marrow (okay, that's just gross) out of each class they attend. But as I noted earlier, if you flat out despise Statistics and resent that you need to take it to complete your major there's only so much self-brainwashing you can do. Again, if you don't enjoy a class it's hard to kick its ass with any real gusto.

So if you find yourself in this scenario (and elect not to take the community college route suggested above) it would be a good time to investigate whether you can take the class on a pass/fail basis at your college. If so, maybe the decrease in stress will actually allow you to experience some pleasure in taking the course. (Unless it really does blow, like Statistics.)

Most colleges permit you to take a certain number of units on a pass/fail basis, but you need to understand the rules and consequences of doing so. Here are some key issues to consider:

1. You may not be able to take particular classes pass/fail depending on your major and/or honors program. (If there are certain defined "core requirements" for obtaining your degree you are probably bound to take those the old-fashioned "ABCDF" way.)

2. If you have your heart set on transferring from community college[2] (or any college) into another college you need to ensure that the courses you are taking pass-fail there (or any course, for that matter) will be credited to your transcript at your future school.

3. Beware of relaxing too much in pass-fail classes. Don't take for granted that you will pass because it's simply not true. Let me paint you an ugly picture: You go insane, forget everything you learn in this book, and blow off your pass/fail class. In other words you fail to pull even a lousy "C" and you end up making a high "D." Now that's bad enough. But guess what grade usually goes on your transcript when you fail a pass/fail class? At some places, you'll actually wind up with an "F"…as in "F**ked." In other words, they won't even give you credit for your pathetic

"D"! What a *horrible* outcome! So every time you get tempted to under-study for your pass/fail class, you had better look yourself square in the eye and have yourself a real "come to Jesus" talk. After all, you will still want to do well. That way you can feel relaxed and confident about all of your classes. Remember: Your objective in every class is to *kick ass*. A pass/fail class is no exception. **Do not consider a pass/fail class to be an invitation to shoot for a "C" or you are courting disaster.**

Do yourself a huge favor and get informed about your pass/fail options through your course catalog and by meeting with your academic advisor, as we'll discuss.

Summer Semester Classes: A Cakewalk ... Or Your Funeral?

Let's say that you're still worried about that Statistics class you must take as a requirement of your degree plan. You've already arranged to take it pass-fail and you've even decided to take it at the local community college. Is there anything else you can do to add another spoonful of sugar to make the medicine go down? Yes ... possibly.

It is generally the case that summer semesters are shorter than those during the school year. In many cases, it simply isn't practical to cover the same ground during an abbreviated summer class. Yes, the class may meet for longer hours to compensate for this rushed schedule – but your Professor may still end up demanding somewhat less of you during this lazy summertime course.

Still, you must investigate this angle for each specific class before you assume it to be true. It is quite possible, for example, that a particular professor will treat a summer class like the Bataan Death March, forcing you to work much harder – *precisely* because you have less time in the semester. Pay a pre-registration visit to the Professor and ask, straight up, "What are the differences, if any, between the summer version of the class and the fall version? For example, are there the same number of tests? Do you cover the same amount of material?" If she asks you why you are so curious simply explain, "I was considering taking the class during the shorter summer semester–but not if it would put me at a serious disadvantage."

That's probably better than saying, "I wanted to take the class in the most sissified version possible so I won't wreck my G.P.A." (even though that's what you mean).

Chapter II

Cutting Through The Crap: Why People Are Willing To Spend Thousands To Earn A College Degree

Key Points

1. The average college graduate earns 74% more pay than the average high school graduate.

2. Attending college but failing to obtain your college degree is not a realistic path to success.

3. Performing well in college shows employers that you are capable of mastering a system of rules.

4. Investigate the ways you can obtain easy "A's" or credits by testing out of classes. (Visit **www.kickasscampus.com** for more information.)

5. Use community college, pass/fail and summer semester strategies to preserve your G.P.A.

Chapter II Notes

1. Coined by John Edwards, Democratic vice-presidential candidate in 2004.

2. By the way, those in rough financial straits can sometimes save money by taking their first couple of years of undergraduate education at community college. There are situations in which this is necessary for folks with limited resources and I applaud their initiative to fight for their education by adopting this strategy. Some even encourage this approach on the theory that nobody really cares if you don't attend the college from which you ultimately receive your degree for all four years. But I don't consider this path to be ideal. Presumably, your college of choice offers better resources and, in most cases, a higher quality of education. This is not to denigrate community colleges or the many fine instructors who serve them – only to say that community institutions are generally not as well funded as other colleges and universities. They cater to a more varied caliber of student under a generally non-competitive, open-enrollment policy. My hope is that you will get settled in your final college destination as soon as practical. You don't want to find yourself wandering from school to school when you could be building a cohesive and, frankly, more impressive record at one place.

There are a lot of people at College who will try to hold you back. If you're not careful, you may be one of them. —**G.F.**

Chapter III

Gunnar's Philosophy Of Intellectual Horsepower

Are You Breaking Curves Or Just Breaking Even?

Two kinds of students will read and benefit from *Kick Ass in College*. The first group bought this guide to get an edge on the pack. These students may be brimming with self-confidence, and eager to break curves and break hearts. Fair enough. There are crucial lessons for them within these pages.

My other group of readers probably do not identify with the confident, empowered student I am telling them they will be. I understand this skepticism. But to them I say this:

I will show you the handful of critical techniques and approaches of people who succeed brilliantly in college. They are not complicated or mysterious. They are easily modeled by anyone with a desire for success. They mainly involve advanced planning, high-quality information, and a discipline that will grow naturally from the seed of success planted early in the span of a college career.

But first, let's talk for a minute about your brain.

Understanding Your Potential

I'm sure you've heard that the human brain is capable of processing an unfathomably vast amount of data, putting even the most advanced computer to shame.

But on a basic level, the brain works like a crude muscle. If you exercise it with moderate discipline, it will produce results. You don't need any advanced software or memory upgrades … you just need to give it a fair chance to do its work.

Working out the old brain muscle.

Unfortunately, many students fail to take advantage of the simple way in which the brain works. Rather than working in a steady, disciplined manner, they place unreasonable demands on their mental faculties, usually around exam time. They also rely on hopelessly inefficient study and memorization methods. Frustrated and depressed by their perfectly understandable lack of success, they conclude that they simply "aren't smart."

The stress these students experience obscures the fact that they have not really given themselves a chance. They mistakenly conclude that they have been putting forth their best effort all along. The truth is, they may have, in fact, been thinking about their problem subjects all along. They have, in fact, been punishing themselves all along. **But suffering is not studying.**

What are the two primary reasons students have difficulty in college? That's easy:

(1) poor study skills, and/or

(2) poor time management.

With some practice and discipline you can ensure that you're kicking ass with the A students. Trust me, this has little to do with "intelligence" and everything to do with playing the game. Keep reading.

You Were Born With It, Baby!

Studies have shown that 5% of human beings are gifted with genius-level intelligence. Another 5%, we are told, are mentally challenged or hampered by a serious learning disability. So that covers that 10%. But more than likely, you fall into the remaining 90% of the population. Sure, some people in this large majority have special talents, like doing arithmetic in their head, playing piano, or creating haunting likenesses of NASCAR drivers using glitter and household glue. But tests have demonstrated that those in this large 90% majority of people possess comparable intelligence. That's right, *comparable intelligence*. Roughly equal...More or less the same....

By the way, you earned your spot in this 90% bracket when you were around three, back when you started using language to communicate. Researchers at The Efficacy Institute point out that **the complexity involved in mastering even basic communication skills far exceeds the complexity of most of the**

kinds of tasks people claim they are unable to perform as adults. From the mouths of babes issues an incomparable feat of intelligence.

How can infants do this? First and foremost, it is their intellectual birthright to be wonderfully intelligent, sophisticated thinkers in-the-making. Moreover, as you've probably noticed, a baby does not harbor a fear of embarrassment or of making mistakes. In fact, babies usually receive constant encouragement from those around them whether they are making progress or not!

A human being's intellectual progress and development after infancy is less certain. As they grow older, most individuals don't have the same opportunities to exercise their minds in this optimum, supportive setting. For example, they may grow up with negative messages about their self-worth. They may be told both directly and indirectly by teachers or by society as a whole that they cannot excel in school because of their economic or ethnic background, or due to some other ridiculous reason.

If they internalize these messages, such persons may reject academic work and other impulses for self-improvement out of fear of failure and embarrassment. In this scenario, an individual's intellectual gifts may remain dormant for the rest of his or her life. If, however, a person is taken out of a non-supportive, resource-starved, mentorless environment and instead bathed in the sunlight of encouragement, some amazing things happen. **Testing of such supposedly lower-I.Q. people seems to show that they actually "get smarter."** Of course, this flies in the face of the premise behind "I.Q." (intelligence quotient) testing since we are all supposed to be saddled with our I.Q. at birth. At the risk of giving I.Q. testing more credibility than it even deserves, let's crush that theory into a fine paste now.

It will not surprise you to know that, without exception, countries plagued with mass poverty have lower average I.Q. scores than nations where the standard of living is higher. If a child isn't given a meal or two of decent food to fuel the brain, that means the little tyke is going to be in for some tough sledding. But it doesn't mean he's a dumbass.

In fact, research shows that one's "I.Q." is *not* static or unchangeable. If you mix "lower-I.Q." children with "higher-I.Q." children, teach them *all* well and place the same high expectations on each member of this mixed-I.Q. group, they will all come to earn high I.Q. scores. Why? Because our innate potential, as measured by some invented test or otherwise, is always far greater than any of us can ever exhaust in one lifetime. In the end, your brain is sort of like Silly Putty® .... You can "Bounce It, Stretch It, Snap It, Shape It, Mold It & Store It in An Egg."

"But Gunnar, What If I've Never Kicked Ass In School? Do You Really Expect Me To Start Now?"

Yes.

Okay, so on a practical level, how does all this feel-good mumbo-jumbo apply to you in college? Consider this: a university study concluded that only *5 to 25 percent* of a student's performance in school was based upon natural ability. The reasons for the remaining *75 to 95 percent* of his or her performance were **"unexplained."** Okay, the "Bermuda Triangle" is unexplained. The success of World Championship Wrestling is unexplained. *This* we can explain. It's not exactly a shot in the dark to conclude that some students are getting better information and support than others.

Successful people might prefer to think that it was their "superior intellect" (as opposed to their educational opportunities, socioeconomic advantages or other factors often beyond their control) that made their academic triumphs possible. Our current way of thinking about success and achievement encourages educators to designate individuals as either "smart" or "dumb" – success-oriented or failure-prone. I once subscribed to this flawed view myself. I figured I had gained admission into fancy schools because I had been lucky enough to be one of the "smart" ones.

But I always had a sneaking suspicion that if underperforming students knew what I had been taught by my academic mentors about playing the college game, they would catch up. Turns out I was right.

* * *

You may be wondering where I get off telling you how to run your life. Well, as I've already mentioned, I served as an academic advisor and curriculum consultant at a large university. My first major assignment was dealing with a group of students experiencing severe difficulties in college.

As you can imagine, these students had extremely low self-confidence. They felt demoralized by their lack of success in their classes, and by the impersonal atmosphere of a large university. By the time they walked into my office, they had usually resigned themselves to failure. They were just waiting to receive their failing grades so they could go home in shame.

How do I know that my kick-ass strategies can help you? Because they are the same strategies that helped students who had all but lost the desire to stay in school. Do you think these students believed I could help them? **Hell no.**

Some students are more receptive than others.

As it turned out, I had to do more than teach them how to do well. I had to teach them how to *want* to do well. I realized from my many meetings with them that these kids were all "smart." And why not? They were all part of the 90% bracket. I knew that nobody with a supercomputer for a brain should be struggling for their academic survival.

Over the course of a semester, I pinpointed three false beliefs that most of my academically troubled students had in common:

1. *Most people who do well in school are obviously smarter than I am.*

2. *I'll never be good at certain subjects.*

3. *Once I mess up in a given class, I will not improve no matter how hard I try.*

You may not feel as underconfident as these students did, but you may relate to some of their concerns. The way these students eradicated these false beliefs was through the introduction of three new beliefs:

1.   Poor performance in the past does not equal my potential ability.

As I have suggested, no one ever even approaches full use of their natural human intellectual ability. All college students already possess the intellectual tools for success and will never exhaust the resources of their mind. The human brain will not fail any student who gives it a reasonable chance to do its work.

2.   I can succeed at challenging subjects through course-correction.

Successful students do not allow themselves to be defeated. They assess their efforts and try new strategies until they succeed.

Unsuccessful students often adhere to the mistaken view that successful students are practically *born* with the right answers.

It is helpful to remember that when NASA fires a rocket into orbit, rocket scientists must make continual course corrections so that the craft follows its proper course. The engineer does not think, *"Gee, the rocket isn't doing what I wanted. I guess I have failed.... You know, I never much liked rocket science anyway."* Instead, if the rocket veers too far east, the engineer sends up course-correction instructions to bring it west. You can and you must use course-correction in your own life.

3.   Competence will give me confidence, and confidence will give me competence.

Your goal must be competence, or a feeling of comfort through skill and practice, in every subject you tackle. As your competence steadily builds, your comfort level will increase, and you will gain confidence. This "virtuous circle" will allow you to achieve a high comfort level in any subject. The trick is just to study with steady, reasonable and daily discipline.

Remember: cramming is never the way to build competence. (We all do it from time to time but it's no way to treat yourself.) Things are much easier when you break them down into their component parts at a reasonable pace. But the only way to experience that level of ease and comfort is to allow yourself plenty of time. This book provides specific strategies to achieve competence, confidence and ultimately, success.

Cramming: Not a good strategy.

Achieving success in college is no mystery. Apply steady effort, proper study techniques (patience, they're coming) and course-correction and you will reap rewards.

Chapter III

Gunnar's Philosophy Of Intellectual Horsepower

Key Points

1. Give your brain a chance to do its work and it will not fail you.

2. Suffering is not studying.

3. Good study skills and time management are far more important to success than so-called "I.Q." or natural ability.

4. Cramming is a recipe for failure.

People like to say that "hindsight is 20/20." But they rarely mention that foresight can also be 20/20. Good planning will give you the foresight to shape what is to come. So why guess the future—when you can create the future? —**G.F.**

Chapter IV

Choosing To Succeed By Planning To Succeed

A Focus On The Future = Motivation In The Present

The number one difference between a person who succeeds and one who doesn't is the quality of his or her planning.

Without a plan, motivation—the engine of success—is not easy to ignite. Plans and goals give context to hard work. I'm not going to lie to you. Hard work is the basis of success. Period. But...

With a plan, hard work becomes satisfying, meaningful work. You begin to require it in your life, like a race horse requires hard riding. When hard work translates into tangible results and rewards, it ceases to be something to be avoided like so much pointless suffering. In this sense, success gets easier to accomplish.

A good plan, broken down into realistic, manageable steps, makes it possible to visualize successful results. If you can see, feel and taste the results of your plan, you will live and work with enthusiasm and purpose.

Remember this principle as you pursue your education:

Plan your Work and **Visualize** your Goals.

You'll see this theme throughout this chapter because it's damned important.

Now it just so happens that I have saved you a *ton* of time and thousands of dollars in books, tapes and CDs. For over a decade I have studied the greatest authors and motivators on the subject of effective goal-setting. I have now distilled and condensed this mountain of information into just a few pages of high-octane motivational fuel. It's powerful stuff so I strongly suggest you read it while seated on a couch or something. If you should feel euphoria or perhaps a slight tingling in your scalp as you read this chapter, *don't worry – that just means it's working.*

Plan for greatness.

The Blindfolded Archer

The famous Zig Ziglar, the great grand-daddy of goal-setting, uses a marvelous analogy to explain why goals matter so very much.

Imagine the greatest archer of all time – capable of hitting a bull's-eye, then splitting his first arrow with a second arrow, and again with a third one, and so on.

But even with such amazing skills, this archery champion could not hit the target if he were blindfolded, spun around a few times, and then pointed in the wrong direction. Sounds obvious, right?

How could an archer hit a target he cannot see?

Okay then…

So how can you hit a target you do not have?

The method you use to set your goals is the method by which you take aim at the target. Is your aim steady and true or are you shaking all over the place? Are you even looking at the target at all?

Good goals, accurately and thoughtfully created, will get you good results. With no goals, or badly devised goals, you'll wind up shooting arrows at your own ass.

Are you aiming for a target?

Goal Power

Studies show that the power of written goals is nothing short of amazing. One particularly famous 1953 study surveyed Yale graduating seniors and revealed that only three percent of them actually had a set of written goals. Researchers tracked the progress of this three percent and discovered an astounding result: each member of this tiny group went on to accumulate **ten times** the amount of wealth as their average classmate in the ninety-seven percent majority! Holy cow!

Again, while money may not always be the best way to "keep score" of one's success and happiness, this should inspire anybody to put pen to paper.

Why does actually writing down your goals work? First, because this act of *conscious focus* counteracts our natural tendency to coast or drift through our days, letting our lives happen to us rather than leaping at the chance to take firm command of our destinies. **Your supercomputer brain is an awesome tool–but you must tell it what to do!** Just a little dollop of daily focus on our goals makes an astonishing difference over the course of a day, a week, a month, a year–*a life.* When you combine written goals with a logical plan to achieve them (as I'm going to teach you to do here) you are suddenly locked on target.

Another reason simple goal-setting works is that it harnesses the power of one of the most potent weapons you have: your subconscious mind. This hidden part of your intellect is nothing less than your own personal miracle factory. As we'll discuss later, your subconscious mind is constantly at work carrying out your conscious goals, even though it's operating under the radar. But if you don't exert control over it can also sabotage you by pointing you in the wrong directions.

Now then, I want you to …

LIST Your Goals ...

Seriously .... Do It.

Your first step in your journey through college should be a very basic assessment of your goals.

For starters, take time to write down 5-10 goals you want to fulfill during your college years.

Next, write down another 5-10 goals you want to accomplish after graduation.

When you write down your goals, free your mind to dream. Some of your goals may seem far-fetched to you now. Don't let that stop you from writing them down. The only limit in this exercise is your own imagination (and applicable state and federal law). Go ahead and write, I'll wait....

I mean it. Write down your goals. Relax and write something down – you will refine your goals in a minute. You can (and must) always revise your goal lists later. Right now we just want to spill some ink and get some ideas on the page.

Okay, okay, some of you aren't writing.... So let's make a deal. Could I get you to put down your goals if you could use a fun computer program to do it? I got you covered. For your FREE *Kick Ass in College*™ Future-Shaping Software worth $49.95 just send an email to:

gift@kickassincollege.com

Refining Your Goals The S.M.A.R.T Way

Now that you've rounded up a stableful of your wild, untamed hopes and dreams it's time to direct them just a little bit. The "S.M.A.R.T." concept[1] is my favorite approach because it ensures that your goals are realistic and attainable. Here's how it works....

Go through and refine your goals so that they are:

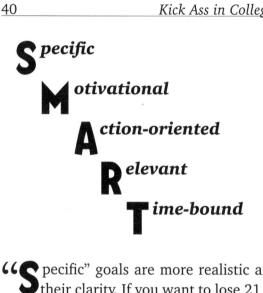

S pecific

M otivational

A ction-oriented

R elevant

T ime-bound

"**S** pecific" goals are more realistic and attainable by virtue of their clarity. If you want to lose 21 pounds, your written goal must state that specific target.

"**M** otivational" goals are exciting goals. They can't be so modest that they are hardly worth achieving. Don't undershoot the target!

"**A** ction-oriented" goals effect some kind of important change – they do not simply maintain the status quo. Such goals are also mapped out step-by-step, and require consistent and steady effort. (As we'll discuss shortly, a crucial part of your action plan must be to anticipate and list all likely obstacles to your successful completion of the goal.)

"**R** elevant" goals are *your* goals. Don't try to achieve somebody else's goal. The "R" might also stand for "realistic" – your goals can be highly ambitious while steering clear of being insanely unattainable. If your goal can be broken down into manageable, realistic steps, then great, even improbable things can happen. An obese person can lose 100 or even 200 pounds. But if that person's ultimate goal is to be a race horse jockey and they also happen to be six feet tall – now they're coloring way outside the lines.

"Time-bound" goals are the only kind that get accomplished consistently. Such goals make a real impact in a measurable time frame (within one week, by tomorrow, by December 15th, etc.). To maximize your success and honor your full potential you must internalize the idea that "a goal without a deadline is just a dream."

So let's look at some examples of **S.M.A.R.T.** goals:

"I will be accepted into the Honors Government Program at the end of two semesters."
That one isn't bad.

"I will improve my grade point average in Russian to an A- by the end of this semester."
Also not bad.

"I will obtain a summer position working for a veterinarian by April 15th."
Hey, you're getting good at this!

Anyway, as you can see, these goals are all specific, motivational, action-oriented, relevant (we'll assume for this exercise) and time-bound. Notice that "I will improve my grade point average in Russian to an A- by the end of this semester" is much better than "I will do better in school." "I will achieve a 3.8 G.P.A. this semester," though more general, is still good because it requires you to make a balanced effort in all your classes.

Of course, the goal must also be reasonably challenging – pushing you somewhat beyond what you perceive to be your current limits. So if you're already making a high B+ in Russian then it's time to shoot for an A, my friend. Don't coast or you'll backslide. You need to seek out challenges to keep you sharp and interested. Otherwise, your subconscious mind may actually start to *limit* you!

Notice also that our model goals are written using the phrase "I will" instead of "I want to." This specific phrasing kicks your subconscious mind into high gear by convincing it that your goal is a *fait accompli* (which is French for "in the bag"). Your brain will then start to nudge you to achieve the goal, like an insistent Australian Cattle Dog nudges a cow into a pen.

Again, don't forget to include any health goals you have such as losing weight or kicking the smoking habit. As time passes, make sure to expand your list of goals, and to check off those you have achieved.[2]

Gone Fishin'

Ageneral word about grades. You're going to kick ass now. What does that mean? Quite simply, there are only A's, B's and C's from this point forward. We don't even think about other letters. They are stricken from the alphabet forever.

I think we understand each other.

And guess what? You'll never accept a "C" again because a "C" will quite simply be a failure in your mind. From here on out you are more likely to see Bigfoot or a unicorn than a "C" on your report card. In fact, if you ever make less than a "B+" again you're going to go down swinging, sweating, and bleeding.

Why? Because you're on the hunt for Great White "A's"– the mighty sharks of the academic ocean. You aren't fishing for canned "B" tuna, and certainly not for measly "C"-sized guppies.

Remember this as you embark on each class: You are a highly trained professional. You are going out to sea and coming back with an "A." It's going to be big and it will have a lot of teeth. It will fight you and test you. But you are going to catch it and it will be yours.

Jump the shark!

Oh, The Obstacles You Will Face!

Most things worth doing in life aren't easy. Get used to the idea that in life we are "entitled" to nothing... You will *always* encounter tough obstacles as you pursue your goals. But if you pin your ears back, dig in your heels, square your jaw, clench your fists, and steel your gaze... you will look like a robot. (It's true.) Besides that, you will experience the sweetest of all rewards: the pride and dignity that can only come from working hard and doing something for yourself. Feel genuinely sorry for those who never experience that.

With some careful forethought, you can create an unshakeable will to master yourself and the world around you. By anticipating the obstacles you encounter as you progress toward your goal you will not only alleviate stress – you may actually prevent these obstacles from ever emerging.

In particular, try to anticipate de-motivating (or even depressing) thought patterns to which you may have fallen prey in the past. As an example, consider some of the self-sabotaging internal dialogues set forth in Chapter III, and then review the clear-headed logic we used to erase and rewrite this negative self-talk.

Remind Me Again Why I'm Busting My Ass?

Another easy way to lock onto your goals is to keep fresh in your mind both the good you will experience by succeeding and the bad you will avoid by succeeding. So this is what you do:

(1) Make a list of the **benefits** you will receive by achieving each of your goals;

(2) Make a list of the **negative consequences** you will avoid by achieving each of your goals.

If you are a human (as opposed to a cyborg like seven-time Tour de France Champion Lance Armstrong) there are times when your motivation will wane. But your personalized reminder summaries will help keep you focused and strong when you face the inevitable bumps in the road on the way to success.

Get It Into Your Head: Programming Your Brain For Success

The next thing I'd ask you to do is to post your list of goals somewhere you can read them twice a day – in the morning and at night. Next to your mirror where you brush your teeth or over your alarm clock are great places. If you're worried about somebody seeing your list, tape it to the inside of the drawer where you keep your toothpaste.

Think of reading your goals as "downloading" your success program into your brain. Ideally, you should also close your eyes and take a couple of minutes simply to imagine yourself fulfilling at least one or two of these goals. Think of this quick visualization process as "running" the program.

I know this practice may sound a little odd but repetitive visualization is a favorite tool of world class athletes. Why? *Because it actually works.* (Pro athletes don't have time to screw around with techniques that are ineffective.) For example, next time you see a football game, watch the placekickers pacing the sidelines. More often than not they are deep in thought as they imagine themselves splitting the uprights with a perfect kick.

The most effective visualization is one that is so clearly and crisply detailed in your mind that it–whatever "it" is–feels familiar and real enough to touch. Think of some positive experience you've had in the past. Your visualizations should seem every bit as realistic as that memory of your past accomplishment.

Goals + Visualization: Your 1-2 Punch

When you couple visualization with the powerful exercise of reviewing your goals for just a couple of minutes a day you program yourself for greatness.

A great example of a successful person who used these techniques is the amazing Jim Carrey, the Jerry Lewis of our time. In 1987, Carrey was a struggling, barely known comic. That year, he decided to give his aspirations renewed focus. He actually sat down and wrote himself a check for $10 million dollars, thus memorializing his **goal** to be paid that sum as a performer. Carrey dated the check for Thanksgiving of 1995 and stuck it in his wallet, where he could view it frequently.

But he didn't stop there. Carrey also began parking his car on Mulholland Drive, far above Los Angeles, where he would look down on Hollywood and spend time **visualizing** his future success. Over the next eight years Carrey radically improved his act, taking the steps necessary to win over the public. We all know the rest of the story. In 1995, Carrey was paid $10 million dollars to star in *The Cable Guy* and continues to enjoy the success he so richly deserves.[3]

Think of how many potentially successful people out there never properly focused on success. Don't be one of them. In large part, success is simply a decision to focus your energy on a goal.

Take A Step-A-Day Toward Your Goals

Here's another key aspect of goal-setting: **Try to take a clear step toward completion of at least one of your mid- or long-term goals every day.** By no means does this need to be a huge step. If one of your goals is to get an internship at an advertising agency you might read an article in a trade magazine to deepen your knowledge of the field, or place a phone call to make a preliminary inquiry at one of your targeted agencies. (It is a good idea to create a list of major action items needed to satisfy each of your goals.) Just imagine your cumulative progress through such modest daily efforts!

Your Daily Goal List: Jump-Start Your Day The Night Before

Each night before hitting the sack, write a quick, practical list of goals for the next day. This will keep important assignments and appointments fresh in your mind and give your day a sense of purpose and direction from the moment you wake up in the morning.

This is remarkably easy if you ritualize it. Just keep a note pad by your bed and scribble into it for a minute before you crash. No big whoop. But it's just a few little extras like this that will make you a force of nature in college.

Who's In Charge?

We are the sum of all of the decisions we make and the goals we set. The decision to set a goal is an internal one–it is a deal you make with yourself to improve your life. Of all the excuses for not pursuing your goals, the most crippling of all is waiting around for external changes before making an internal decision...

"I'll figure out my major eventually. Something will hit me sooner or later."

"That financial aid counselor was supposed to phone me last week. Hope she calls before registration so I can figure out how I'm going to afford tuition."

"I'll get on an exercise schedule as soon as my roommate gets organized. That way we can go together."

One word: **Lame.** Never wait for somebody else to do something before you attack your goals. Excuses are for losers. Don't go out like that.

How's Your Temperature?

Here's another reason to be deliberate about setting your goals... Ever notice how some people can't seem to rise beyond a certain level of success, financial or otherwise–or fall below a certain level of failure? It's as if they have an internal thermostat that tells them they're too "hot," or too "cold." And so they subconsciously strive to be in that comfort zone of averageness and mediocrity. The simple practice of *writing down your goals* (or typing them into the free *Kick Ass in College*™ Future-Shaping Software) is a way to take control of that thermostat and ratchet it up.

Maybe you've never felt as though you belong in the same league with the "smart" students raking in the A's. But your list of goals will mold your consciousness and raise your expectations.

We know that higher expectations lead to better results. As you read on you will understand exactly how "A" students operate. You will have the will, determination and information you need to live out your goals and rip that thermostat right out of the wall. You will learn, out of habit, to continually challenge your own perception of your comfort zone. Then you will look behind you at the trail of success you've left in your wake and think, "Wow! Did I do all that?" Get serious about your goals. It is a practice that will serve you well throughout your life.

Don't Hate ...
Congratulate. Appreciate. Celebrate.

I've alluded to it before but you've got to populate your world with similarly motivated and goal-oriented people. You may wish to share your goals with your good friends. Just be careful because, unfortunately, it is usually easier to find people who will not support you (and who may even try to sabotage you) than to find folks who can rise above their petty jealousies.

Expect the best out of people but don't be surprised or disheartened when they turn out to be full of crap.

Chapter IV

Choosing To Succeed By Planning To Succeed

Key Points

1. With a plan, hard work becomes satisfying, meaningful work.

2. Use the "S.M.A.R.T." system to document your goals.

3. Use the same visualization technique as pro athletes.

4. Surround yourself with goal-oriented people.

Chapter IV Notes

1. There are several versions of the "S.M.A.R.T." paradigm. It is likely that the first version appeared in a book entitled *Attitude is Everything*, by Paul J. Meyer, which I highly recommend.

2. Some people like to create weekly, monthly, annual, three-year, five-year and ten-year goals. This is a phenomenal practice, but do me a favor and just get into the basic habit with a handful of goals as I've suggested above.

3. I feel compelled to point out that Carrey also *loves* his work. Anybody can see that. The money he is paid is a powerful affirmation of his talent and gifts. But to such a performer a big payday is secondary to his pride in his craft. If, on the other hand, you are a person *"who seeks only silver, then you will never be satisfied with silver."* That's from the Bible, and the same sentiment is expressed in the Torah, the Koran, in Buddhist and Hindu scriptures, and so on. If you choose your major, take a job, or make other life decisions based solely on money with no regard for what's in your heart, or simply to please someone else, you may never find the peace to enjoy the fruits of your labor.

If you're doing things the hard way, or thinking about things the hard way, doing and thinking harder will not get you any closer to your goals. —**G.F.**

Chapter V

Making Them Eat Your Academic Dust The Gunnar Way

Here's The Deal

The next couple of chapters cover study skills. You'll find some kick-ass study tips here, as well as some essential advice to help you get your mind right. You won't know what hit you but you will know one thing: **Gunnar Fox is an F'ing Genius.**

It's important for you to know that for a particular tip to be included here it had to be:

(a) highly effective;
(b) something you'll actually use; and
(c) something you'll actually use consistently.

People are always full of bright ideas, like telling you to draw lines down the middle of the page when you take notes for God-knows-what-reason, or insisting that you should use six different colors of highlighters. I'm not here to overwhelm and demoralize you with outlandish tactics you'll never apply. This chapter is supposed to make your life *easier.*

Again, if you see a tip in here it made the cut because it's field-tested and practical.

What Professors Really Want

Briefly stated, professors want students to do one or both of the following:

(1) memorize a lot of facts; and

(2) demonstrate a command of the material sufficient to permit you to form arguments, draw conclusions or obtain solutions using these facts.

In short, professors want some pain. They are nice enough folks, but they want proof that you've learned something from them. We're going to give them that proof.

During the course of a history lecture, for example, a professor will paint a panorama of people, places, events and dates. When it comes time for the teaching assistant ("T.A.") to grade an essay exam, he or she will likely be referencing a list of people, places, events and dates that could have, or should have appeared in your essay responses. The T.A. will read through your essay, placing check marks next to these specified objects of memorization. You can write a beautiful essay, but if you do not list enough memorized facts in such a class, you're sunk. Along these lines, always err on the side of **volume** in your essay answers and in general. You will get a higher grade than those who give skimpy responses.

Of course, it's not enough merely to memorize a crapload of facts. That, by itself, would merely be "surface learning." You also need to lock on to "deep learning." *Deep learning means truly understanding that which you are memorizing.*

Professors want some pain.

If you don't understand the material it's much tougher to retain. If you ever feel as though you are not on a clear path to deep learning – even in the very first week of class – consider it to be an emergency situation, like a grease fire. Sure, it may not be a four-alarm bonfire … but you wouldn't want to turn your back on a flaming skillet in the kitchen would you? That's the vigilant mentality you need to bring to this college thing when you see even a spark of trouble.

Learn to recognize an emergency situation.

The nice thing is that mere repetition – surface learning – constantly improves your ability to achieve deep learning. In fact, *everything* I teach you about the mechanics of kicking ass in college leads to deep learning.

Good Students Keep Up. Great Students Stay Ahead.

College students are constantly facing huge waves of information rolling toward them, threatening to crash on top of them with all of nature's fury.

"C" students find themselves flatfooted, drowning in the powerful undertow.

"B" students are overwhelmed by the waves but have learned how to keep their heads above water.

"A" students find the discipline to stay slightly in front of the waves, surfing ahead gracefully and maintaining control to the end. How do they do it? It's all about doing just a little more than the rest of the pack: **Budget the time to read ahead in your class text or, at a minimum, just skim ahead by one or two assignments.** Your understanding and retention of class lectures will increase significantly. I'm talking about a relatively small sacrifice that yields disproportionately high returns. The confidence and peace of mind that results from developing this habit of surfing ahead a bit will improve your quality of life by 17.5 percent.

Kick Ass Early And Often

Along the same lines as above, you will reap massive rewards if you hit the books like a maniac for the first two weeks of each semester. If you can destroy your first couple of quizzes and build a firm foundation for each of your classes, this will create powerful motivation to continue to stay ahead for the remainder of the term.

While others hang loose, chill out, and generally bask in the memories of simpler, pre-college times on the beach or at the mall, you do your thing – quietly and humbly focusing like a laser on your first few assignments. Setting a positive tone at the beginning of the semester is another discipline that yields HUGE benefits.

Attend Class As Though Your Grades Depended On It ... Because They Do

S tatistically, class attendance is one of the most important factors in determining what grade a student will receive. By failing to attend class you shortchange yourself in multiple ways.

First, you deny yourself the heart and soul of the college experience. You might as well go to one of those online universities or send off to some offshore diploma mill for your degree. Studying may be a principally solitary endeavor but class time is designed to be quite the opposite. It is there that the give-and-take of classroom discussion allows you to benefit from the wisdom and knowledge of the instructor while honing your own communication and public speaking skills.

Class lectures are also the forum in which to benefit from the combined intellect of your classmates. Colleges make extraordinary efforts to improve the caliber of their student populations through building state-of-the-art facilities and providing other enticements.

Skipping class hurts you in more concrete ways as well. Some professors penalize or even fail students for poor attendance. Absent students also fail to pick up the professor's cues for what will be emphasized on tests. A missed class is also a missed opportunity to better memorize the material by hearing it discussed out loud.

"A" students attend class religiously. Simple as that. There is no valid rationalization for skipping class short of grave illness.

Despite what the mediocre student wishes to believe, it *will* hurt you to miss class. Don't believe the hype from those who claim they don't attend class or even study. Let the braniac know-it-alls do it their way and you just stay the course. Others' unwise or freakish behaviors are irrelevant to you.

My biggest key to getting good grades at college was just showing up. Ordinarily, poor attendance is every frat-daddy's Achilles' heel. I managed to drag my happy ass to class every day and it made all the difference.... Also, these egghead professors, truth be told, are insecure. Their little feelings get hurt when you don't show up at class to listen to them pontificate.—**N.C**

You Can Hear The Crickets Chirp During Office Hours

Do you know why professors and teaching assistants often use their office hours to read the paper? That's because few students –let's call it 5%–ever take advantage of this time to get help or ask questions. It is not unheard of for a professor who teaches a class of 400 to sit alone in silence during the two-hour block he or she has set aside for one-on-one consultations with students.

You must schedule frequent opportunities for personal contact with your professors and teaching assistants. At least three times a semester is a good benchmark.

These meetings will enhance your knowledge of the material and potentially give you the inside track on what is coming up on future exams. Your interaction with professors may also provide you with a valuable reference for the future. (More on getting references later – just file it away for now.)

Most faculty members enjoy answering questions when a student comes well prepared. What does "well prepared" mean? It means that your questions are neatly written out, and that you have already done your best to find the answers for yourself. Don't waste your instructor's time by asking questions you could have easily answered after glancing through the syllabus or your class notes.

What will you discuss? What questions should you bring? That's easy. How about these for your first meeting (they won't all apply but they'll get you started on the right track)...

Your professor is waiting... and waiting... and waiting.

(1) "Can you suggest any strategies for mastering the material? Do you recommend any outside reading to enhance students' understanding of the lectures?"

(2) "How much of a time investment do you anticipate the highest-performing students will make in preparing for the course on a weekly basis, roughly speaking?"

(3) "Are there any pitfalls students should avoid in taking your course?"

And here are a few that could work for subsequent meetings ...

(1) "Could we discuss a few of the errors I made on the last test/ homework assignment?"

(2) "How might I improve my next essay?"

(3) "Do you have suggestions about graduate school or career op- portunities in your field?"

Anyway, it's not hard. Just make sure you ask any follow-up ques- tions – don't stick so closely to your script that you miss opportuni- ties to clarify things the professor has said in her answers. Whatever you do, avoid being pushy or aggressive or clever in trying to get hints about what will be on this quiz or that test or you'll just piss her off.

Once you have built some rapport the professor may suggest that you emphasize certain topics as you study for upcoming exams. Just because you are enthusiastic and conscientious they may just break you off a little sumthin' sumthin' to help you out. This will prob- ably give you an unfair advantage over your classmates. How can this happen? Simple: **Because life's not fair. And you know what? It's not going to get any more fair.**

In years to come you will receive higher pay from your boss, better loan rates from your banker and fancier haircuts from your stylist – all because of your successful attitude. People will say, "Boy are you lucky." But luck will have nothing to do with it. Just be grateful you know how to conduct yourself. And be generous in advising those who come to you for advice on how to improve their "luck."

By the way, if you make an appointment with a professor – keep it. Some professors have a policy of refusing to give appointments to students who have already missed an appointment without a legiti- mate excuse. Along these lines, be sensitive to the instructor's time constraints. If you are organized and sharp, you can be out of there in

10-15 minutes. If the professor decides to ramble on about unrelated topics, just to be social, you should be honored and listen politely, hanging on every word. It's all part of a successful interaction.

Lastly, be prepared for rare instances in which you will need to wait your turn to speak with the professor, such as before an exam. Always have your **spare-time study materials** handy so you won't be idle during this time (more on this later). As my favorite fortune cookie says, "Idleness is the holiday of fools."

Life Is Too Short To Take Sh*tty Classes

I have had some dazzling, even legendary professors in my day. I always blew the lid off of those classes. It felt like an honor to be in the presence of such luminaries and I was inspired to do my absolute best.

I've also had a couple of real duds who should never have been allowed to teach Defensive Driving much less Comparative Religion. I don't recall ever earning any particularly outstanding grades in those classes.

While mediocre teaching is no excuse for a mediocre effort on your part (everybody is dealing with the same boring or unreasonable instructor) you should make sure your schedule is dominated by daily opportunities to be amazed and amused. When you are enthusiastic you have the best chance of performing at your peak. I have to admit, it took me a while before I realized I could take control of the quality of my instruction rather than simply leaving it to dumb luck.

When you skim through your college course catalog you get only the most basic information about each class – name, rank and serial number kinda thing. What you need are the **departmental descriptions** of the classes, which will provide you with three key pieces of information:

1. An in-depth description of the class.

2. Whether the class will be tested using multiple-choice exams, essay exams, term papers, or some combination.

3. The name of the professor teaching the class.

A thorough description of the class will help make sure you get what you bargained for. If you prefer to write essays or research papers instead of multiple-choice tests you can refine your selections on this basis as well. Most importantly, you will need the professor's name to check out his or her **teaching ratings** and **awards**.

Finding this information may be as simple as looking online at your school's website. Or you may need to walk to the relevant department where course information is posted. The campus activities office or student union (or wherever the student government offices are) are good places to start looking for information about professors. You may also be able to learn about grade distribution in a particular class so you can avoid professors who are unreasonably stingy with A's. Also, don't hesitate to ask more senior students for their opinions as well. College is no time for shyness, folks. If you stumble blindly into a class taught by a raging hardass it's your head on the block.

Just make sure you ask veteran students relevant questions about the class. ("Professor Sullivan is a hottie" may be a plus but don't end your research there.) And needless to say, don't base your judgments on one or two opinions. You never know if somebody's just got a case of sour grapes or some other major malfunction. Recognize that there are plenty of students who don't put in the hours but would prefer simply to blame the professor for a poor grade rather than take responsibility for blowing off the class.

Registration: In It To Win It

Make sure you complete class registration as soon as you possibly can.

For example, if your school requires you to sign up for classes by phone or email start jamming the circuits the minute registration opens. When I was in law school, certain classes taught by "celebrity" professors only had room for ten or twelve students. To have a chance at a brush with fame you had to be physically present to sign up at 8 a.m. on the day of registration. *Everybody* wanted to get in. But my roommate and I apparently wanted in worse than the other 1000 would-be entrants because we always found a way to sneak, ninja-like, into any class we wanted. How? On the eve of every semester, the night before sign-up, we would literally camp out in front of the registration office and spend the night there in sleeping bags. When 6 a.m. rolled around, dozens of students would show up, assuming they would be first in line, only to be disappointed. A little extreme? Yes. **But if you remember one thing from this book let it be this: Successful people aren't normal. They do what other people don't, won't or can't do.**

Okay, but let's say you identify a class you want, but for whatever reason, it's full to the gills. Don't give up! If you've only asked once that's not enough by a long shot. Inquire to the department about whether you might be able to squeeze in if somebody else drops the class. If all else fails, go and speak to the professor. But first type a brief letter to him or her explaining your reasons for wanting to join the class. Cite your interest in the subject matter and your eagerness to experience award-winning instruction. The point of this exercise is to show the professor that you care enough to go to some effort to earn a spot in the class. By the way, *don't* just write an e-mail. Email is convenient but it will not make the same impact. If your college has a pure luck-of-the-draw internet registration system, that's all the more reason to make the process as personal as you can.

It's The Little Things...

A s suggested by the letter-writing gambit above, it is a well-known technique in sales to give prospects a small gift in exchange for a bit of their attention. This creates a mild sense of obligation – which can actually be annoying as hell if not handled properly.

But just a bit of soft-selling may make the difference in any number of situations. As the semester progresses and you have developed a pleasant rapport with the professor, little things can make a difference in how you are perceived. Let's say you go on an interesting trip. What's the harm in writing the professor a little postcard? (Don't forget the T.A.) Sound cheesy? Put yourself in the professor's position. We all like to get nice postcards. I've sent them many times and they are always received well. Just don't lay it on too thick. A simple salutation ("Best from Toronto" or "Fond regards from Prague") is a nice gesture.

As the years pass, a small gift would reinforce your regard for the professor as a mentor (perhaps a book or a DVD might strike the right tone), and maybe as thanks for a glowing reference. Curiously, one professor I admired greatly once asked me if I would serve as a reference for him after he was nominated for a $10,000 dollar teaching prize. I did and he won.

You can guess who I asked to write my references for law school!

If you find a great professor who thinks that you hung the moon, and the feeling is mutual, take every course he or she offers. This prof will be your mentor, your future senior-thesis advisor and the author of the recommendation that will be your ticket to your dream graduate school. If he went to your dream graduate school, so much the better. (Just don't disappoint him by going to law school instead.) —**K.L.**

Drop It Like It's Hot

Despite your best efforts you may ultimately end up in a hideous class. My advice should be superfluous at this point: **Get Out**. Quickly.

You may still end up paying for the class if you fail to drop it before the end of the grace period for such changes but it may be well worth it to take the hit. Better to figure this out as early as possible, though. That way you finalize your schedule and get on track immediately. Don't make the mistake of holding on to extra classes and "auditioning" professors for extended periods, hemming and hawing and wringing your hands about which ones to keep. Given that you must *stay ahead* in all of your classes keeping extra classes is a recipe for disaster. By the way, make sure you know exactly when the "drop date" deadline is or you'll be in a world of hurt. (See your course catalog or official school calendar.)

If you wind up being stuck in the class (it happens) find a way to be successful. Don't complain–**study**. And try to figure out what makes the professor tick. If the instructor is a crashing boor or a prickly fascist, then you'll have a little more trouble making a connection, won't you? But connect you will because getting an edge is your job.

Take Note

Everybody takes notes a little differently, and that's fine. There are all kinds of variables to consider, such as the instructor's lecture style, whether the material from the lecture closely tracks the text, and what style of notetaking makes it easiest for you to recall the material at a later date.

Here are some guidelines I believe are the most practical:

1.   **Get to class on time.** Not just because it's rude to be late, and to make sure you don't miss anything. The real reason is because you need a moment to get situated in your chair – so you can take a deep breath and FOCUS on why, exactly, you are there. If you are feeling tired or a little de-motivated this is especially important. By making a quick mental effort to remember one or two key reasons why your education is so important to you, you'll energize yourself and get in the proper

mindset to take good notes. (Whether that means imagining your dream job as Secretary General of the U.N., or buying a Porsche Cayenne in "Rich Bastard Red," that's on you … whatever thrills your grill.) As explained below, going to class must not be a passive exercise. Sure, some of your classmates will look comatose and barely even there. Their notes will look sparse and, frankly, useless. But you're on a different plan. You know that the time to relax is *off* the clock. You'll have plenty of time to kick back after you've put in a day of work that will make you feel justifiably proud.

2. **In most cases it is unwise merely to "listen" to lectures as opposed to taking notes.** Good notes are the spine of most classes. They are your connection to the best source of information regarding what will be tested. Your mission for each class is to come away with excellent notes. It is not always easy to do this. Sometimes you might not feel like exerting the effort. But it's your job and a very worthwhile task.

3. **Use abbreviations in your notes and generally avoid writing in whole sentences.** But, I would suggest that you not take this too far. Sometimes, students try to be so economical and efficient in their note-taking that they can't make heads or tails of what the professor said. My own advice is to push yourself to take fairly detailed notes. In fact, I don't hesitate to write in complete sentences when I want to remember the professor's exact words. Sometimes a burst of added detail helps take your mind back to the day of the lecture, sharpening your recall. A lot of people tell you to write down just a few words *"so that way you can just listen and take in the information."* That's horsesh*t. Don't be lazy. You'll be thankful you took great notes later.

4. **You may have some opportunities to summarize concepts as opposed to writing down the lecture verbatim.** But again – be careful. When students hear a lecture for

the first time they don't always summarize the material so well on the fly. Sometimes the professor (a) writes something on the board or (b) gives you a cue that something important is being said, such as *"This will be on the test"* or *"To summarize"* or *"Let me repeat"* or **"Write this down you boneheaded dorks."** When this happens, again, don't summarize jack–just write down every word. Why? *Because often, the instructor is using these cues to put the most important ten percent of the material on a silver platter for you.* Professors rarely "hide the ball," okay? Most like to unfurl big red flags to help you focus on the stuff they're going to test.

5. **Supplement your notes by trading with a classmate who seems to be on the ball**–preferably someone who is also sitting near the front row and can recite huge chunks of *Kick Ass in College* from memory. Just be sure you make copies (or back up your files) before entrusting anyone with your notes or any other product of your hard work.

6. **You'll take better notes, write more neatly, stay more alert and make a better impression on the instructor if you sit attentively and avoid slouching.** Assume an "attack posture" in class, alert and forward-leaning.

7. **Use the memory enhancement techniques covered in Chapter X to make maximum use of your notes.** Good notes are the ultimate memorization tool.

By the way, notice that my study system is simple–and realistic. Some academic "experts" overload you with tedious techniques that no one would seriously incorporate into their study routine. If you truly want to kick ass, you've gotta keep it real.

No Such Thing As Extra Credit

It pays to complete all "optional" extra credit assignments. While purportedly optional, such opportunities to garner free points are always tackled by the best students. What does this mean? Simply that anyone who wants to run with the big dogs who score the A's can't afford to skip extra credit.

Since *you* are gunning for A's you've got to be all about extra credit. The advantage of completing these bonus assignments usually goes beyond scooping up some precious bonus points (which would be reason enough to do it). The fringe benefit is that the professor is providing you with a means to improve your mastery of the material beyond the ability of most students. This will pay dividends on future tests when this material reappears.

There is one exception to this rule and that is when the professor issues a virtually impossible challenge for extra credit. This should be pretty obvious from the dizzying nature of the task or question presented (I think we all saw *Good Will Hunting*). In this scenario, give it a shot but don't kill yourself over wacky brain-teasers at the expense of following your normal study routine.

Get With The Program

Consider joining some sort of academic "honors program" as soon as you can qualify. This deserves a spot on your list of goals for college. Do not be intimidated! The higher your expectations for your own success, the higher your level of success will be.

If you have never thought of yourself as an "honors student," start today. All freshmen start with a clean slate with regard to their G.P.A. If you were a B student in high school use the techniques in this book to reinvent yourself and become an academic star. As you've seen, being a great student has far more to do with *how* you study than it does with killing yourself in the library or some mysterious gift beyond your control. If you apply these study methods (tricks, really) in college, you will come to be considered an honors-caliber student in a matter of one or two semesters.

If you can hit a certain G.P.A. target you can become eligible to participate in an honors program of some kind. This gives you access to your college's best professors and resources and makes for an impressive tribute to your scholarship on your resume and/or diploma.

Most colleges have an honors-track curriculum that corresponds to your major (or your minor, should you elect one). For example, you can graduate with a plain-Jane "English degree" or you can earn your degree from the "University English Honors Program for Literary Badasses."

Front-End Tutoring: Getcha Some

Let's say you have math issues. Maybe math doesn't get your blood pumping. Maybe you even have a math phobia. And let's say you're going to have to take some math in college to fulfill your degree requirements. In other words, you are expecting some turbulence ahead and your dread and anxiety are growing. I couldn't feel more strongly about what to do in this situation. **You must arrange to be tutored at least once a week – not after you get in trouble but *before* you do.** It is critical that you get this kind of tutoring right smack at the beginning of the semester.

How can you get tutoring? Let me count the ways....

1. Your teaching assistant or professor may be able to meet with you for regular tutoring help. This may be the ideal situation – IF you can get sufficient and consistent help in this way.

2. You may qualify for free tutoring at your college or university through the academic counseling center or the office of the dean of students.

3. Student honorary societies and other organizations may provide free tutoring.

4. You may be able to perform tutoring in a certain subject (or provide some other service) *in exchange* for help in another subject. Place an ad on campus bulletin boards if this is the case. (Alternatively, solicit volunteers to come to your aid. You may be pleasantly surprised by the ample goodwill of your peers. Again, just don't be a "study mooch" by failing to return the favor in some way.)

5. You may be able to afford to pay for tutoring. But be wary of price-gouging companies that may offer shoddy and uninspired tutoring. Give them a try but don't hesitate to drop them like a bad habit if you aren't benefiting. Graduate students may also be available to assist you at the rate of $15 to $30 dollars an hour. Again, don't waste time with somebody who isn't Johnny-on-the-spot excited to be helping you.

I recall an incident when a tutor paid by the University was caught sneaking off with his tutee to watch porno flicks instead of helping the young lad with his astronomy. Depending on your point of view, this is probably not the way to get the most out of your tutoring. You have to make sure your tutor is motivated to teach you the material. In fact, if they aren't a total nerd who lives and breathes the subject, get somebody else. —**S.T.**

Don't think of tutoring as something you seek out in order to go from a "D" to a "C," but rather as a means to locking up an "A." **Another important incentive for you to seek out tutoring: It will save you time.** Sometimes you can get more done in an intense tutoring session than you can in four or five hours of bloodying your nose on the grindstone by yourself – or in a primarily social study group (see below).

Study Groups Vs. Study Buddies

Study groups may also be helpful, at least on a limited basis, but be wary of wasting your time with students who are not as serious or productive as you.

Study groups in college are great… for meeting women.

—T.B.

In fact, if you study well with others, I would advise you to seek out no more than one or two other like-minded individuals to work a class with–conscientious people who are not merely looking to be carried to the finish line. They say two heads are better than one but that's only true if both heads have a brain.

Never forget, however, that the vast amount of your studying should be done alone. Tutoring and study buddies can be critical but there are two primary ingredients of study success:

(1) You, by yourself; and
(2) Plenty of **"B.T.C."** (Butt To Chair).

Tutoring Your Friends: The Perfect Disguise For A Selfish Act

If you really want to cement your knowledge in a class then tutoring a struggling buddy every once in a while might just be the Krazy Glue® you seek. You don't want to spend huge chunks of time baby-sitting and hand-holding but this can really take your own knowledge to the next level. We'll cover how such selfish acts of generosity can boost your essay-writing ability a little later.

I remember taking an upper-level math class that was pretty esoteric. Two hours before the test, a hysterical and ridiculously unprepared friend asked me to help him "study." Since there was no real time for much studying, I looked over my notes and identified a portion of the lecture in which the professor explained a logic tree for systematically solving each of the types of math problems we had covered in the class to date. Over the next frantic hour, we reviewed this diagram, which my friend managed to memorize. We then tried to work through a couple of relatively simple problems, but it was clear that he was having a great deal of difficulty. He was screwed, right? Under these dire circumstances, he marched in with me to take the test. The professor proceeded to hand out blank sheets of paper and announced that the entire test would consist of one question: "Diagram the logic tree for systematically solving each of the types of math problems we have covered in this class to date." Needless to say, my friend did extremely well on the test; in fact, he got an "A." More importantly, so did I! Which leads me to the two points of my story. First, teaching others is often an effective way for you to learn. Second, there is nothing wrong with helping others even if you are "competing" with them for grades. Generally, your help will be rewarded. —**H.S.**

Your Study Corner: Get Your Daily P & Q

Seek out a place to study at the library. Find a secluded corner and deliberately associate that place with studying. This corner should have a proper desk, a good chair, consistent temperature and plenty of light (by a window may be even better). Most of all, it should have plenty of **"P & Q"** (peace and quiet). Don't plant your flag by the copy machine or the elevators or anywhere likely to attract a lot of distracting traffic.

Never allow yourself to lose concentration or fall asleep while you are in your study corner. If you feel your mind wandering, or Mr. Sandman tugging on you to take a siesta, take a walk or a leak or *something*. But NEVER allow yourself to do anything but study in a focused manner in your study corner.

It's worth repeating: The vast majority of your studying should take place in your library corner, primarily in solitude.

Create the perfect study environment.

You should also have a **secondary study corner** at your desk in your room, which you should think about in the same way, with the same strict rules. Don't forget the bright light[1] and the quality desk chair.

The Sound Of Silence

Do not listen to music while attempting to study. This practice slashes your ability to absorb and memorize information (yes, studies have shown it). Either you listen to music or you study. Don't try to make studying more enjoyable with music or listening to music more productive through studying. You'll only diminish the value and effectiveness of both activities.

If you find that you are easily distracted by noise, or if you need to experience some peace and quiet in less-than-ideal study conditions I recommend you visit the Bose® website at www.bose.com. There you will find a line of amazing noise-canceling headsets, which you may have previously tried while on an airplane (certain airlines permit you to borrow a pair to decrease the sound of the jet engines during international long-haul flights). There are less expensive brands available at your local computer or office supply store (or at www.sharperimage.com) but this is one of those areas where you seem to get what you pay for.

This technology will allow you to avoid the stress and frustration associated with trying to ignore annoying sounds, especially in a high-pressure situation in which you might otherwise kill somebody with your bare hands.

These headsets also provide superb sound for those times when you do want to listen to music.

Highlighters: Modern Miracle Or Instrument Of The Devil?

First things first on this thrilling topic. Yellow is a unique color because it offers high conspicuity (it stands out against most anything) and high contrast (it's easy to see dark colors against a yellow background or vice-versa). So don't bother buying any other highlighter colors because they aren't as practical.

Think of highlighter ink as the most precious fluid in the universe, to be used ever so sparingly, and only late in the study process. If you use highlighters on a first read-through of a document or book you have a tendency to over-highlight – thus totally defeating the purpose. You may also fail to highlight the information that will be most useful to you.

How, exactly, do you know what is going to be "useful" in the text? It may take a little while. First, you will need to get a sense of what the professor's areas of emphasis are as revealed (i) through class lectures and (ii) through your conversations after class and during office hours. Second, you will need time to get a sense of more obvious concepts on which you need not waste your precious golden-yellow fluorescent elixir. Thus, only when you have a firm sense of the material should you unsheathe your mighty highlighter.

Having said this, I do believe there is value to "active" reading. Many students also intuitively understand the value of trying to pick out key material and then carrying out the mechanical act of putting marks on this information. This is why I recommend marking up or underlining the text (sparingly – let's not get carried away) with an erasable pen or automatic pencil you can easily erase, unlike a traditional highlighter.[2] The side benefit of using a pen or pencil instead of a highlighter is that it forces you to be alert since it takes slightly more effort. When armed with a big sloppy highlighter you have a tendency to paint the whole page with a blinding coat of yellow. That's *not* active reading. You barely need to be conscious to do that.

You should also make notations in the margins, especially when you see something you intuit will be tested. Later you can come back and do your highlighter thing if it helps you embed the information in your memory.

Let me also make a point to those of you who aim to keep your books pristine so that you can sell them back. While I applaud your thrift I think it's penny-wise, pound-foolish in this instance. Marking up your books is a part of the learning process you should not deny yourself. (In any event, you should be able to sell back books that are not in mint condition, at least at a discounted rate.)

On the other hand, don't buy used books if they are plagued with somebody else's notes and highlighting. This could quite possibly end up annoying you to death.

Your Library: It's Not Just For Books Anymore

Look into taking a library tour. Few students ever learn about all of the resources their college or university library features, much less how to use them. Learning about your library's computer research tools is itself worth the price of admission. Just ask the librarian. No biggie.

Upgrade Your Head Weekly

It's not a bad idea to reserve one hour each Sunday morning to read a newspaper. I like the *New York Times* Sunday edition. You may prefer another paper, but make sure they put out a decent weekend summary of the week's news. If you can afford to subscribe, great, otherwise, hit the library. (The reason I am *not* suggesting that you read the paper daily is that I do not consider it realistic or even necessary if you are consistent on Sundays.) I am also a rabid fan of a magazine called "The Week." It offers you a quick and dirty weekly summary of the news as covered by the world's best newspaper editorialists and cartoonists. You can even read it on the treadmill (takes about 25 minutes) and you get enough balanced information to satisfy even a hardcore news junkie.

When you come into class armed with knowledge of current events, you can make a genuine contribution to discussions, and your courses take on added relevance to your own daily life. It is a tragedy that our generation is killing the newspaper industry because we don't read the news. Successful people from Birmingham to Bucharest consider the newspaper to be required reading, and so should you.

Supermodels

As simplistic as it may sound, there are formulas for success. If you identify successful students, you can discern certain similarities in the way they pursue their college education. See if you can figure out who (other than you) is making top grades. Watch how they behave with teachers. Sneak a look at their notebooks to see what they are writing down. How do they spend their weekends? If you play your cards right, they'll share their wisdom with you.[3]

Get to know these experienced and savvy students and model them.

Pick their brains for advice and the inside, scoop on professors. *What should I take? Who should I take? What organizations should I join? Boxers or briefs?* They're bound to tell you something useful. By the time you've studied the habits of four or five of these hot shots you can create your own success formula. Don't reinvent the wheel if somebody else is already riding on 24-inch Sprewells.

Chapter V

Making Them Eat Your Academic Dust The Gunnar Way

Key Points

1. Professors want some pain.

2. Great students stay ahead and kick ass early.

3. Never miss class – unless you are hospitalized or something.

4. Take advantage of your instructor's office hours – but prepare in advance.

5. Take responsibility for getting classes with the best professors.

6. Go to extremes to register for the classes you want.

7. Remember the power of a postcard.

8. Be an active note-taker, not a lazy listener.

9. Extra credit is never optional.

10. Join an "honors" program A.S.A.P.

11. Tutoring is your secret weapon.

12. Avoid unproductive study groups.

13. Most of your studying should be solitary—just you and "B.T.C."

14. Get your daily "P & Q."

15. Highlighter ink is precious. You can purchase erasable highlighters and other great gear at **www.kickasscampus.com**.

16. Knowledge of current events enriches your class experience.

17. Model the Supermodels.

Chapter V Notes

1. I prefer OTT-LITE® light bulbs, which simulate natural daylight (www. ott-lite.com). These special bulbs give off an energizing, mood-elevating light, and are exceptionally gentle on your eyes. They aren't cheap but last many times longer than ordinary bulbs. If you want to try a less expensive brand you can search the web for "full-spectrum lights."

2. I suggest you purchase one of the coolest school tools ever: the ink-Tank™ erasable highlighter by Binney & Smith, the people who brought you the Crayola® line. Love this product! Visit your local office supply or **www.kickasscampus.com** if you'd like to purchase some.

3. You may be surprised to discover that some of these academic stars in your classes are older, so-called "non-traditional" students returning to school after time in the workforce or raising a family. Often, they have a lot of incredible life experience under their belts. Equally important, they exhibit a level of motivation and maturity worth emulating.

Don't f**k up. — **G.F.**

Chapter VI

Averting Disaster: There's More Than One Way To Flunk A Cat

"Freshman Paralysis":
Coming To A Slacker Near You

Each fall, as students trek off to college, a devious monster waits in the wings, ready to sweep fresh student meat into its lair. Its terrifying but unwieldy name is **"Freshman Paralysis."**

During the transition to college, freshmen must adjust to a new place, to new people and to new responsibilities. No longer will the student live within a structured family setting, with set wake-up times, bed times and meal times. Nor will the student's clothes get mysteriously washed, folded and deposited in drawers. Most importantly, no one will be breathing down his or her neck to roll out of bed and into class.

These changes in your life all fit under the category of **freedom,** which is at once exhilarating and scary. With all of your newfound freedom you may feel disoriented. Disorientation can develop into the feeling that you **"don't belong"** – as though a freakish clerical error somehow landed you in "The Valley of the Brilliant and Well-Adjusted." At this point you are especially vulnerable to Freshman Paralysis, which may first lull you into submission by playing on your insecurities. Everyone around you appears to know exactly what they are doing and why they are doing it. Even those in the restroom seem to attend to their business with particular intensity and purpose. About this time, maybe you start to feel a twinge of **homesickness**.

Freshman Paralysis can zap you early and never let you go.

To cope with these feelings of "not belonging" you decide that all you need to do is meet some more people. Go to a few parties. Go to more parties. This is the way to fill this void of alienation, right?

Wrong. Unfortunately, Freshman Paralysis has you just where it wants you. Now that you are softened up it will hit you with the most common emotional byproduct of the transition to college: **debilitating procrastination**.

Procrastination is an insidious obstacle to the academic progress so critical in the first weeks of college. Commonly, procrastination manifests itself in avoidance of class work in favor of **"escape sessions"** with similarly paralyzed students. You may party too much. You may watch T.V. too much. You will almost certainly **"do nothing"** too much.

Most freshmen who get into early academic trouble say they were

"academically overwhelmed." But upon further scrutiny of their study habits, they may concede that in their efforts to cultivate a lively social life, or to "belong," they blew their grades.

This desire to be social is understandable. Many students are away from home for the first time and eager to explore the outer limits of their freedom (specifically, to go on a "Hunk Safari" or "Beers of the World" tour). It is remarkable to see the effect that such a sudden increase in freedom can have on even the most diligent, mild-mannered freshmen – especially if they are still resting on their laurels from a sterling high school record. As a result, even some Valedictorian types screw up big-time by mid-semester. Be forewarned.

Ultimately, Freshman Paralysis can land students on **scholastic probation**. If they do not moderate their habits and slay this beast, they will definitely feel like they do not belong because they really won't. The Dean of Students will expel them, thereby relieving them of the responsibilities they had earlier opted to put on the backburner.

Freshman year at UCLA the RA[1] gathered us in the common room of our dorm for his own special version of freshman orientation. He said, "Over half of you will not graduate four years from now. Some of you will be drop-outs. Some of you will be five-year Seniors or even 'permanent students' with long white beards who will be here for decades. Nevertheless, I'm going to tell all of you something right now: There is no excuse for not graduating with flying colors in four years. This place is idiot-proof if you are sincere about wanting to graduate." I don't think the good people at UCLA would want their school to be known as "idiot-proof" but that's beside the point. He had me pointed in the right direction from Day One. — **S.M.**

Focus Slays The Beast

The day you set foot on campus, your feelings and actions must be ruled by one powerful idea: *I am an important and vital member of this college community and my success is my first priority.*

Sound silly? I guess talking to yourself is, in a way. But it is essential that you continually affirm this idea in your mind in order to maintain your **focus**. Focus is the silver bullet that kills Freshman Paralysis dead.

Focus now! Before it's too late!

Remember your goals list? Keep it handy. Know your goals intimately. Focus on your goals accurately. Act on your goals aggressively. Don't let anything or anyone derail you.

The Three Most Important Letters In The Alphabet: "C.Y.A."

Always get important representations made to you by counselors or administrators in writing. This is known as a **"C.Y.A."** ("Cover Your Ass") memo – a frequent tool in the professional world.

People are funny. Some speak confidently and know nothing. Others seem wishy-washy but they are totally reliable. You just never know.

Ideally, important degree requirements and school procedures are already documented in printed school guidelines found in your course catalog.[2] But if they aren't, and when it really matters, see if the college administrator you are dealing with will put it in writing for you.

If nobody wants to type a note for you, type it yourself to the particular bureaucrat's satisfaction and have them sign it. Never rely on anybody blindly when your academic career is on the line. Make a habit of checking things out for yourself. The famous actor Ronald Reagan put it best: *"Trust but verify."*

A familiar 16th century proverb tells us that "the road to hell is paved with good intentions." Don't let well-intentioned people in college administration give you bad advice. They'll usually be right, but not all the time. Politely protect yourself when dealing with people in authority because nobody else will. Otherwise, you can bet you will lose the "your word against mine" showdown if things ever go south.

Friends Don't Let Friends Bug The Crap Out Of Them When They Are Trying To Study

Almost inevitably, your friends (or so-called friends) will try to pressure you to blow off school when you know very well it would be unwise. You must say **NO**, early and often. This may make them angry at first, but if they care about you, they will deal with it. You may even influence them to study more, although this is not your job. Recognize that you are not doing yourself or your friends any favors when you cave into their unproductive demands.

Serious study means getting away from phones and visitors. Nothing can be more detrimental to your efficiency than having people make demands on you while you are trying to work. Be forceful about asserting your right to study from the start and your efforts to achieve success will be respected.

The Reward System

Remember: Fun social events, mixers, movies, T.V., going to concerts or sporting events, and other diversions should be RE-WARDS you give yourself for kicking ass in school. As a practical matter it's hard to have fun if you're not on top of your class work anyway. That's like the mental equivalent of walking around with a backpack full of bricks.

Rewarding yourself for hard work and a job well done, on the other hand, is a beautiful thing.

Cribs: Choosing Your College Housing

Where you live in college can make an enormous difference in your success. One off-campus apartment building at my college consistently had the highest freshman drop-out rate while another boasted a perennially high average G.P.A. among residents. Well guess what? My advice would be to choose the second place.[3]

Your choice of college housing can have a
direct impact on your G.P.A.

There are plenty of factors involved in making this decision but if you've read this far you have enough sense to figure them out for yourself. Here are just a few issues I would highlight as you undertake your housing analysis:

1. **Movin' on up.** If you plan to live in a dorm, inquire about "Honors Floors." An important aspect of your quality of education (and of your quality of life, for that matter) will be the people with whom you live. Honors Floors should afford you plenty of peace and quiet, as well as more good resources for help with the occasional late-night question. If you live with people who study, you will study more. If you live with people

who start boozing by noon or stay up all night vegging in front of the T.V., you may be tempted to join in. Moreover, these people may pressure you to stop being such a "loser." (And by "loser," of course, they mean "future boss.") *What are you trying to do, anyway? Get high grades so you can have the career of your dreams?* Gee, if that makes you a loser sign me up.

2. **Choosing a roomie.** If you are asked to fill out a form so that you can be matched with a roommate, explicitly ask for a real bookworm. You know, a real Sherlock von Einstein type. There are a couple of strategies that will serve you well as you go through this crazy life and one is to s-t-r-e-t-c-h. Not just in the sense that your reach should always exceed your grasp, or that you should shoot the moon when setting your sights. You must also stretch by meeting gifted people who are different from you – *really different,* if possible. Your choice of roommates is one such potentially enriching opportunity.

Another life strategy is to always play the game with people who are better than you. Ever played tennis with somebody really talented and find that you play out of your mind because they bring out the best in you? Again, look to your roommate for that kind of experience and try to provide it for him or her in some area if you can.

Whatever you do, be practical. If you live with someone whose temperament and personality does not allow you the option of sleeping at night and studying in your room when you need to, your life will be hell. If you find you've been assigned to live with some freak or jerk-off who really starts to affect your academic career, just switch rooms – it happens all the time. (Unfortunately, splitting the room in half with a strip of silver duct tape won't solve the problem.) Don't be shy about it and don't hesitate. Just take the steps necessary to get out of Dodge and don't let the door hit ya where the good Lord split ya.

If your roommate sleeps all day, neither bathes nor changes her sheets, and keeps weeks of fast food remains in the bed with her, this is not a case of "free to be you and me." Maybe they have a case of major depression, or some other serious ailment. It's up to you to get her help when she starts to fall apart (even if you can't stand her). The same is true for serious substance abuse, bulimia, firearms, and other threats to personal safety. Otherwise these kinds of problems frequently bleed over into your own life. — **W.W.**

3. **How about living at the frat or sorority house?** Not a big fan because you aren't likely to get as much exposure to the non-Greek community, and because of the traditional emphasis on throwing the best blow-outs. But there have been a lot of successful folks who've gone through school as Greeks so there may be ways to make it work for you. Most such organizations have a member dedicated to maintaining academic standards and monitoring mandatory study hours. It would be helpful for you to *become* that member or to assist with those duties to maintain your scholarly focus. Similar issues exist for student athletes. Just make sure you avail yourself of all of the academic resources your school offers, as we'll discuss later.

I attended a small college in Kentucky. Unlike many in my fraternity house I was a bit of a study geek. If I couldn't get to the library it was always a challenge to find a quiet

place to study in the house. The best place turned out to
be in a sitting area near the entrance. My dear sweet Mom
built me a lap board to use for studying on the couch. Of
course she made it bright blue with the word "BETA" written
on it in big letters. Not so cool. I caught endless amounts
of grief from my fraternity brothers and male and female
visitors to the Beta house ... at least until report card time!
Bwahahahaaa! Geeks rule!—**K.L.**

4. **If you plan to live off campus**, try to live as near to your
    school as possible to trim valuable commuting time from your
    schedule. If parking on campus is a problem, consider taking
    the bus or riding a bike.

5. **Buying a house or condo?** I am a firm believer in real es-
    tate investment as a wealth-generating and tax strategy (but
    that's another book). If you or your parents are in the position
    to buy a place near your college where you can live for the du-
    ration of your studies it could be a wise investment. But again,
    location, location, location is a key consideration because you
    don't want to be or feel too isolated from the rest of the stu-
    dent community.

6. **Living at home?** Not my favorite approach to tackling adult-
    hood, though financial and other considerations may prevail.
    Were our culture more accepting of kids staying home with
    their parents into their 20's and beyond, as young adults do in
    Latin America, I might have a different view. But to be in step
    with your colleagues it would be a good idea to at least spend
    a couple of your college years under a different roof. You have
    to cut the umbilical cord sooner or later and college is a good
    time to do it, since the next step (full-fledged adulthood) is a
    doozey.

I recall moving into the dormitory as a freshman, and boy was I ever "fresh"…right off the farm, in fact. I was fascinated to learn that my neighbors were two Jewish kids from Skokie. Having never met a real live Jewish person before, I engaged them in many interesting discussions. These guys were hilarious. Once an evangelist came by the dorm one Sunday morning and asked them, "Do you have a personal relationship with Jesus?" They grinned and one of them answered, "Yes. Jesus was my cousin. What do you want to know?" I guess somewhere down the line they really were related. —**A.T.**

I had this roommate from China – or "Red China" as my Dad still calls it. We shared an apartment in some pretty nice (but small) subsidized university housing, complete with a kitchen and separate bathrooms. No matter how many times I complained, my roomie was always pan-frying these smelly fish that were too big to fit in the pan. They still had their heads and tails and everything else, and they gave off massive amounts of pungent smoke as he charred them. Rather than crack a window he would simply disable the fire alarm. After a while all of my f**king clothes smelled like fish. (Other Chinese people I knew on campus would laugh when they found out I was living with him because apparently he was from a small town and they considered him to be really "country.") To be fair I probably also drove him crazy in my

*own way. I used to blast my Nirvana at all hours of the day and night. And once I forgot to lock our front door and lots of our stuff got stolen. Then there was the time my idiot buddies were moshing in the living room and they shattered our front window when it was below freezing outside. Anyway, as the months passed, my roomie and I accommodated each other more and more. In fact, we actually became pretty tight. I learned a lot about Chinese politics and culture, and he got me seriously into martial arts. He also set a great example by studying like a machine (he was a double-E major) and we helped each other with assignments (okay, so he helped me). Long story short, keep roommate relationships in perspective and look for the best in people. And before you bitch and moan, take a good look in the mirror to see what you can change. You'll have some problems living with anybody when space is scarce so be ready to compromise here and there. —***R.M.***

Correspondence, Internet & T.V. Classes: A Bad Idea

I counsel you to avoid any kind of self-study classes. Period. In the first place, they defeat one of the basic purposes of a college education: that you interact fully in live classroom discussion.

But on a more practical level I have never seen students run into more trouble and sweat more bullets than when they are given responsibility for fulfilling assignments at their own pace. These classes are just train wrecks waiting to happen. Even the most disciplined students struggle with this format.

You want to get even more practical than that? These classes often turn out to be a four-legged bitch. Much harder than normal classes and a lot more work.

Theoretically, one could take a class from the convenience and comfort of one's living room couch. But an ounce of practice is worth a ton of theory. And in practice, it's nowhere near as easy as it sounds.

Good Love

Ah yes, College. I remember it well. A time when the thoughts of young men and women turn to love...

It's a thin line between love... and a "D" average.

Some people meet their soul mates in college – that special someone with whom they will share their lives, rocking together on a porch swing for the next fifty years as they reminisce about the day they first met.

But some of you may meet somebody else altogether: a temptress or a charmer who entices you to join in a frenzy of irresponsibility and craziness that sure feels like love – but which ends in an equally spectacular display of hurt feelings, recriminations and broken glassware. But I'm not bitter.

Yes, that swirling, tornado-like sensation of being swept off your feet was actually your life being flushed down the toilet as you neglected your classes, lost your friends and, quite possibly, tattooed your ass with somebody's name. Only after the spell of the passionate infatuation wears off do you realize the relationship had been, well … a mistake.

You may not want to hear this when you are in the throes of young love but no matter how cute, or enthralling, or buff he/she is, you still need to make your education your top priority.

A romantic relationship in college, as in any phase of life, will have its ups and downs. But you must look out for yourself by ensuring that you diversify your emotional portfolio enough to withstand these rough times. Don't allow a romance to dominate your life. Resist the urge to cocoon with your sweetheart in a world inhabited only by the two of you.

These feelings may be thrilling but not even that exhilaration is worth the tragic consequences of a semester (or longer) of poor grades and other serious problems.

Intimate relationships must be built in the context of real-life needs and responsibilities. They cannot be sustained in a vacuum of fantasy and escape. Being realistic and mature about the nature of a relationship can be difficult whether you are 16 or 60, so rely on those you trust to help you keep your perspective. Anchor yourself with friends and family and try not to be offended if they express concerns about someone you are convinced is the Second Coming of Sliced Bread. Don't ignore the opinions others may provide – just let them sink in and see if they help center you.

If you can't study with your new companion, or if he/she is not supportive of your need to make school your top priority, this is not good love. Enjoy the people you meet but don't sacrifice your future for *anybody*.

Oh yeah, and **don't date your professors** ….

Professors who date their students are serially exploitative, without exception. Even the sad, puppy-eyed, yearning ones. Unless you want to share a warm moment of sisterhood, years hence, with another alumna who fell for the same line from Professor Suave, walk away. — **J.M.**

To Part-Time Or Not To Part-Time...

As you know, you already have a job – being a college student. Your priority is to study and build a strong academic record. I advise that you put maximum effort into applying for financial aid so you can avoid taking on a part-time job to generate income during the school year (and that goes double for a full-time position).

Again, financial pressure can sink college students as easily as academic failure. Tuition price increases are outpacing inflation. Often, a student's knee-jerk reaction is to get a minimum-wage job. But consider this: if students spent *one tenth* of the time researching financial aid as they did flipping burgers they might not need the job at all. When I say "researching" I mean becoming a *stone-cold expert*. Not just skimming a few summary materials. Your financial aid office will have bushels of books that will help put serious money in the pockets of those students who learn how to play the system.[4]

Yes, those who evaluate your record in the future may cut you some slack on your G.P.A. deficiencies if you worked to put yourself through college. But the preferred approach is to do everything possible to earn superior grades since your academics will play a far more significant role in your future than the few bucks you might earn making sandwiches.

Bottom line, if you can borrow the money to attend college, do so.

Your Financial Aid office may be able to provide low-interest loans that you can pay back on generous terms over a bazillion years. (Your eligibility is largely dependent on your parents' income and their degree of financial involvement in your education.) If necessary, take on work during breaks between semesters to make up any shortfall but otherwise stay focused on school.

Lighten The Load!

I f and only if you are convinced, even after in-depth discussions with your financial aid counselor, that you must work to support yourself during college, do not take on a brutal course-load. Why would you do that? **The point of going to college is not simply to "get through" college! It is to *kick ass* in college.**
God Almighty, who are you trying to impress?

Make sure you put together a reasonable mix of classes each semester. For example, you don't want four classes that will all require intensive writing, or four classes that all have lab requirements. If a semester has a few particularly grueling courses, try to balance it with a pass/fail class, or an elective (like karate or some other physical activity to provide some stress relief). —**W.D.**

Graduate From The McJob

T o branch off from the last topic, if you ultimately conclude that you *must* work to support yourself during college, do your best to identify a position that goes beyond burger-flipping or retail sales.

While food service and hawking shoes is hard, honest work that'll keep you off the streets, try to think in terms of finding a job that helps you create an interesting, provocative resume – maybe even something that has some relevance to your career aspirations. For example, if you can snag an out-of-the-ordinary job as an office assistant working at the state capitol, or as an assistant at a nursing home (jobs that may also provide meaningful opportunities for advancement over the course of your college years) you can earn some income while also putting an impressive feather in your cap.

Work-Study: A Real Deal Or A Raw Deal?

If you qualify to receive financial aid you may also qualify to participate in a Government-sponsored work-study program. Tread carefully before accepting such a position because you could really take it in the keister. **Specifically, you may be jeopardizing opportunities for loans and grants.**

The general idea behind work-study (though there are exceptions) is that you forego at least *some* traditional financial aid cash in order to work, thus lessening the amount of loans you take out. But as I've mentioned, my advice is that you not worry about student debt at the expense of achieving the best G.P.A. and academic record you possibly can. (And if you can get grants then you have the best of both worlds – free money and time to study.) Do *not* let a fear of loans drive you to work-study.

The trouble with work-study is that your college will probably only pay you the applicable federal minimum wage, which is only four or five bucks an hour. While you may not be too excited about that your college makes out like a bandit since it only ends up paying you around a dollar and change per hour. Uncle Sam usually picks up the remaining 75% of the cost of your wages.

Okay, so at 5 bucks an hour, working for eight hours means you make $40 bucks, right? **Wrong.** To add insult to injury, you can look forward to paying federal and state taxes on that embarrassment of riches.

I wish that were the only potential problem with work-study. Your college may also have some tough rules that basically prohibit you from dumping your piss-ant work-study job after you wise up. How can they force you to work? By not allowing you to be eligible for loans or grants, at least for the current semester, after you've started the gig. Yes, ladies and gentlemen, forced servitude still exists in America today.

Heard enough? Well here's the last thing: not only are work-study rules sometimes draconian and the wages a pittance – they may not even let you keep the job beyond a certain number of hours. Which means you have to go find a different sucky job if you need more hours.

So maybe it's not all glamour. But for certain people there can be a lot of positives to taking on a work-study assignment. Let's say you aren't quite so strapped for cash (but still demonstrate the need for financial aid, as required to participate in a work-study program). A work-study position doing office work or research for a professor can kill multiple birds with one stone:

(a) you can round up some walking-around money;

(b) you'll likely have an understanding employer who can appreciate the need for you to focus exclusively on school from time to time; and

(c) you have a perfect opportunity to develop a rapport with an influential mentor. Similarly, a job working with one of your school's sports teams may give you great experience and gym access if you are interested in a career in physical therapy or sports medicine. Enough secondary benefits can make a work-study position actually worth considering.

A part-time job in an academic department, even outside your major field, will net you a very respectable reference, worth far more than the one from the manager at Wendy's®. And with a little luck, you'll find lifelong friends and mentors there. — **J.M.**

Read your college's work-study rules carefully so you don't screw yourself out of other financial aid opportunities. Maybe you'll be pleasantly surprised and discover that your college has student-friendly regulations that make work-study jobs especially appealing.

Cheaters Risk Taking It In The Shorts

Make yourself aware of your school's official policies regarding cheating. There will probably be some sort of "honor code" statement on your school's website or in a pamphlet made available to you.

Aside from prohibiting the obvious cheating strategies, many schools, for example, forbid you to use the same paper for two classes without specific permission from both instructors. This is known as "multiple publication." Needless to say, garden-variety plagiarism and its revolting cousin "plagiarizing from an essay you downloaded from the internet" are illegal on every campus.

Some professors also don't want students to use commercial outlines, which I suppose they think encourages the student to avoid going to class.[5] (I would actually file skipping class under "moronic" as opposed to "cheating" per se, since students cheat *themselves* when they do it, but more on that later).

Cheating is not only morally wrong, it is also highly risky. Colleges and universities have become increasingly sophisticated in their safeguards against cheaters, and they will seize upon an opportunity to make an example of someone. (Maybe because of Animal House, college deans have a particular hard-on against fraternities running cheating scams.)

The tired old *"pssst...show me your answers"* ploy still occurs when professors with large classes rely on multiple choice exams. Nonetheless, sharp-eyed proctors roaming the exam hall still manage to nab their fair share of cheaters. And man, is that an ugly scene when it happens. Then there's the old "hire somebody to take the test" gambit. Hard to believe, but people are still trying that one — and getting caught. Trust me, when I worked in the Dean of Students office there was no shortage of those poor cheating bastards begging for mercy.

If somebody went inside your home, trashed your room and stole your pricey sunglasses or your CD collection would you feel guilty about "snitching" or "ratting" them out to the police? In most circumstances, you wouldn't hesitate. Likewise, one of your fellow students might be inclined to point the proctor in the direction of obvious cheating or inform the professor about a stolen test. It would be their right. After all, what price do you put on a semester of hard work? How do you assess the damage done when a block of students mysteriously wreck the curve and you get a B+ (or worse) instead of the A- (or better) you deserved?

Point is, a decision to cheat has a fairly high probability of biting the cheater in the ass, sooner or later. Then what happens? **An academic dishonesty violation will destroy your G.P.A. and tar your academic transcript with a nasty statement that tells the whole world, which includes all prospective graduate schools and employers, that you're a cheat.** Yikes. If you aren't swayed by moral arguments alone maybe that'll give you food for thought. As for those of you who would never dream of cheating, forgive the lecture but this is just about keeping honest people honest. And one way honest people keep honest is by avoiding the horrible desperation associated with losing control of your classes.

As knowing professors like to point out, it takes as much time to cheat effectively–fashioning "cheat sheets" and developing other devious means–as it does to study effectively. Get a long-term edge on those students who cheat, and actually learn the material.

Pulling The Rip Cord

This next comment probably isn't intended for you because it only applies to a very limited number of students. If you experience a serious personal catastrophe (such as the death of a parent) or a medical issue (such as a serious illness or debilitating depression) that renders you temporarily incapable of pursuing your studies and requires you to take a break you *must* follow certain steps:

(1) Document all aspects of your situation or condition, assembling all relevant medical documents.

(2) Meet with academic advisors to ensure that you are not penalized in connection with your withdrawal (or you could quickly destroy your G.P.A.).

(3) Plan to return to school after a defined period of time off.

There is one other scenario in which you may need to withdraw – in which case the same rules outlined above also apply. Sometimes students don't know why they've come to college, or they simply aren't ready to accept the challenge. Maybe it's a maturity issue or maybe they'd rather be in the military. Maybe they really don't have their goals in mind.

If you aren't intensely focused on an ambitious goal, like being an engineer, a veterinarian, a speech therapist or getting your Ph.D. in philosophy (or whatever), it's going to be awfully difficult to muster the necessary motivation to "get your sh*t together," as we say in the education game.

If you are one of these temporarily unmotivated students (you'll know pretty soon if you are) you must act early to preserve your options (not to mention your valuable time and money). It may very well be the case that you will want to return as early as next semester, or perhaps after a productive period of work of some kind. When you do ultimately return (and don't dilly-dally), ensure that you have your goals in firmly mind.

The point is, work the system so that the choice is yours. And make sure you get the terms of your withdrawal and presumed re-admission **in writing** from officials at your college.

Get Off The Fence

My last comment of this chapter is also for a fairly small audience: those would-be students who are trying to decide whether to go to college but who have been sucked into the frenetic world of a McJob, waiting tables or doing some other kind of work that may not represent their life's ambition. They know they want to go to college – perhaps they have even *been* to college for a brief period – but they just can't seem to find the time to get the show on the road.

This book, especially the next chapter, will help you to push through the sludge of disorganization and uncertainty that is holding you back. But for now, just remember that there are only a couple of things you must do to get started on the road to (or *back* to) college:

(1) Get a copy of your **transcript** from your high school (or GED program);

(2) Conduct **internet research** to learn all you can about the colleges you aspire to attend;

(3) **Call the admissions offices** of the colleges you are interested in and make appointment with an admissions officer (a face-to-face appointment if practical);

(4) **Meet with an admissions counselor** to discuss your prospects for admission and any key deadlines for application;

(5) Obtain **financial aid information** if needed, preferably through a financial aid counselor referred to you by your admissions officer.

Make the time. Don't make excuses. Aside from your health and that of your family there is very little, if anything, that could possibly take precedence over getting your education. Live that way and you'll be all right.

Chapter VI

Averting Disaster: There's More Than One Way To Flunk A Cat

Key Points

1. Focus is the silver bullet that kills Freshman Paralysis dead.

2. Always get a "C.Y.A." memo when dealing with college administration.

3. Serious study means getting away from phones and visitors.

4. Use movies, T.V. and social events as a REWARD for kicking ass.

5. Where you live during college matters. *A lot.*

6. Bookworms make the best roommates.

7. Self-study classes are not a good idea.

8. Don't sacrifice your future on the altar of love.

9. Put maximum effort into applying for financial aid to lessen the need to take on a job to make ends meet. Visit **www.kickass-campus.com** for the best in financial aid tools.

10. If you conclude that you *must* work, seek out a job that will benefit you beyond the simple paycheck.

11. Cheating is a losing proposition.

12. If you must withdraw, do so by the book to preserve your options.

Chapter VI Notes

1. "RA" stands for "Resident Assistant," usually a Junior or Senior hired to administer dormitory activities and maintenance.

2. By the way, don't let your college change the graduation requirements on you (for the worse) without a fight. Argue that the rules in place when you matriculated should apply.

3. Whatever you do, just don't try to live secretly in the basement of the library for months on end like that kid from NYU.

4. I urge you to check out the amazing financial aid resources at **www. kickasscampus.com** and start piling up the scholarships and grants today! Your time is precious. We're talking *Lord-of-the-Rings* precious, okay? I would rather see you studying and assuming leadership positions in campus organizations than spending that time at a work gig.

5. If your professor permits the use of commercial outlines, and you swear an oath to use them as merely a supplement (not as a means to miss class or to skip your own note-taking), go ahead. But never try to read more than one commercial outline for a course. Some students try to lay their hands on every possible outline ("to make sure I don't miss anything") and end up chasing their tails. By spending so much time reading other people's work, they neglect to distill and assimilate the subject for themselves. That's no way to earn a top grade.

Taking a test doesn't have to feel like walking the plank.
—**G.F.**

Chapter VII

"Gettin' Testy Wit It": Curing Test Anxiety And Laughing In The Face Of Death

Anxious Before Tests?

T he best antidote to test anxiety is knowing that you are prepared. And whether you are prepared is largely up to you.

You can study in a calm, consistent, savvy manner…or you can cram and choke. It's just that simple. But many students just can't seem to accept the power they have over tests. Their attitude is that test days are always bad days – opportunities to fail. In fact, test days are opportunities to *kick ass*. **Accept control and don't let tests just happen to you.**

You have the power to tame that test.

Brain Fuel

Again, the best antidote to test anxiety is preparation. The best antidote to hurling during a test is not eating like a pig beforehand.

But the real reason not to gorge before a test is to avoid expending your body's energy on digestion when you need to be fueling your mental processes. That said, don't go into a test hungry either. Slam down a boiled egg (or some other form of quality protein) and a slice of fruit and get in there. As a general matter, you want to eat all of your meals–especially on test days. If you skip a meal your blood glucose takes a dive. Since your brain basically runs on glucose, that is not good. Also, do me a favor and walk briskly to the classroom where your test is being held. A little physical exertion does wonders to prime your mental machinery for a challenge.

Testing 1-2-3

Here's a cool way to use your notes and your class text. Go through the information and pick out just the scary stuff. Use that material to make up the meanest test questions you can and drill, drill, drill. (If the textbook actually provides you with questions at the end of the chapters **do them** – duh.)

You will essentially defang and tenderize this tough, sinewy material, which has the highest probability of being tested. Pretty soon, you won't remember what you were so worried about in the first place, and that is a *grrrreat* feeling.

If You Are Worried It Might Be On The Test... It Probably Will Be

If you happen upon a difficult concept in the text, or come to a chart or diagram that is particularly challenging and time-consuming to understand, there is a high probability that it will be on the exam. Just take a deep breath, and dive in.

You always want to study as smart as you can but there are times when you just flat out have to study *hard.* Professors want some pain, remember?

Stop Studying, You're Making Me Nervous!

I used to catch all kinds of grief from classmates when they would see me riffling through my notes just before a test. "If you don't know it by now, you won't learn it five minutes beforehand," they'd whine.

But they were wrong. In the first place I would routinely see something in the last few minutes of studying that would help spur me on in some way during the test. So why not take a last pass at my notes if it might mean one or two extra points?

Second, it was a question of attitude. I was psyching myself up, getting ready to pick off every single question like ducks in a shooting gallery.

Third, you will find that if you get your mental machinery humming along a little early you can hit the exam in fourth gear. Otherwise you're just idling in neutral until somebody hands you the test and you eventually manage to get your head into the subject.

An Old School Technique: Study Old Tests

Here's an idea: **Ask your professor or teaching assistant if he or she has any old tests you can review.** Many professors keep a dusty old test file at the library. Incredibly, students rarely take advantage of this often easy-to-access, solid-gold information. Sometimes, those professors get a little bit lazy and use some of the same questions again. *Schwing!*

*This happened more than once in college: the exam was **exactly** the same as one of the old practice tests. It was like shooting fish in a barrel.* —**B.E.**

One caveat, however, is that you *must* absolutely ensure that any old test you obtain was truly intended by the professor to be made available to you. You want nothing to do with a stolen copy of the actual test to be given or some other shady document not meant for public consumption.

The sad truth is that a few professors – the truly lazy ones – sometimes use the exact questions time and again. The problem arises when they *don't* make their old tests available *and* they know their old tests are floating around out there. It's obviously unfair if only *some* students (*i.e.*, cheaters) will be able to obtain copies through black market networks (*e.g.*, frats or clubs). If you feel you are get-ting screwed, act tactfully and respectfully to see if the Professor will address the situation by providing a set of tests to everyone. Professor Sloth may then tumble to the conclusion that he needs to change things up and stop using the identical questions if you can't benefit from his laziness fair n' square-like.

As a last resort, take it up with the Dean. I have been in this sit-uation myself and it sucks. But you must act to protect your G.P.A. and your future – it's your job.

Use Every Trick In The Book ... And Then Some

Check your bookstore or the web to see if your textbooks have a study guide and/or a teaching edition. These can be excellent, time-saving resources that will help you master your classes. But don't pull the trigger yet...

First, ask your instructors if they recommend (1) purchasing the study guide and (2) whether they feel the teacher's edition would be of benefit. They may tell you that purchasing the study guide is a waste of money because the professor's emphases are different. They may also inform you that students who procure the teacher's edition are actually cheating. If this happens, you can obviously for-get these ideas.

But if they tell you that using one of these study aids is a terrific plan then go out and make the investment.

It is also possible that your instructor may be uncertain as to the value of such publications, never having reviewed them. If so, you may still wish to purchase the study guide and/or teacher's edition as appropriate (keeping your receipts) and ask your instructor to evaluate these materials.

There may also be additional study aids (*e.g.*, online quizzes) avail-able on the internet if your textbook has an accompanying website. I would also seek your professor's comments about the value of in-vesting time online.

Of course, your class notes are your primary study resource. They will highlight at least some of what the instructor considers most important about the subject matter. But there is often other information found solely in the textbook that will also be tested. Also, the professor's explanation of certain topics may be incomplete or unclear and best supplemented through textbook study. For these reasons, the study guide or teacher's version of the text may be powerful resources for elevating your comprehension. After all, these supplements will pinpoint the main themes in the text. This is powerful knowledge that can increase your focus.

Just a little of this highly efficient extra effort per textbook chapter can easily mean the difference between a "B" and an "A."

Unleash Your Subconscious Mind On Exams

Occasionally you will face an exam that requires you to write a number of essays. This happens to be the most common format in law school, where I learned a great technique from a renowned professor.

Even though it might feel a little intimidating, look over the entire exam and read *all* of the essay questions posed before you do anything else. (Make sure you also read the *test instructions* at least twice.) This not only helps you budget your time – it also allows you to multi-task on a subconscious level. While you are using your **conscious mind** working the first question, your **subconscious mind** can be simultaneously working on the other three or four questions.

It will become obvious to you that this is working as you go through the test. As a matter of fact, even though you are focusing on one question, valuable information will start bubbling up from your subconscious mind that is relevant to answering the remaining questions. You may find yourself jotting down a list of thoughts relating to the next questions even as you are drafting your first answer.

This subconscious method may also have applications for a variety of other exam formats. You can quickly skim all sorts of tests and other documents in order to use this uncanny ability, which was included at no cost along with your brain. Just remember that you don't need to spend more than a few seconds contemplating whatever information you want to load into your head. You're just seeking to acquire a basic understanding of the questions presented so your subconscious mind can get crackin'.

Cherry-Pick At Your Own Risk

I've heard people recommend that you go through tests and pick off all of the easy questions first. My experience is that this strategy can be a big time-suck. Students start getting so wrapped up in the analysis of whether a question is "easy" that they (a) squander the exam period and (b) get careless. Don't assume any question looks "easy." That's where they get you. If you blow the answer, it won't matter if it was supposed to be easy or not. If it ends up being easy after careful analysis, great.

Is this a hard and fast rule? No. Just stay on your toes and don't assume it makes sense to skip around on a test like a freakin' jumping bean.

"Stick Around" And Other Tips For Essay Exams

Stay for the entire allotted test period in the case of essay exams or any other exam format. You can always revise and improve your essay answers. (By the way, when you complete your answers write on **every other line** and only on **one side of each page**. That way, you'll have plenty of room to insert or interlineate additional information as you review what you've written.)

You should also create a quick outline of your answer before you dive in to writing each essay. Your outline need not be anything formal with Roman numerals and all of that jazz. Just use a separate piece of paper and list the main topics you plan to address, leaving room to make sub-lists of ideas you want to address under each topic. Update your little outline as things occur to you in the writing process.

This will not only make your thought process more organized, but your work will also look neater.

Since you will probably be writing your essays by hand, you must devote some care to neatness. You may not have beautiful penmanship but test-graders appreciate your efforts to make your answers legible and will reward you for it. You should also use an **erasable pen** in conjunction with a separate **block eraser** since the teensy ones on the end of the pen are quickly ground down to nothing. If you have a nice big eraser at your disposal you can erase more quickly and thoroughly.

Make sure you periodically go back and read what the question is asking you for because sometimes we get so caught up in writing our essay that we forget to give a comprehensive answer. Another way to ensure you've given a complete response is to make a quick list of all of the concepts that relate to a particular essay question. Ensure that you have made some reference to those topics in your answer.

Recall that your professor or T.A. may be grading your essay by literally *counting* how many related topics or dates or pieces of jargon you were able to cram into your answer. Make good use of any extra time by logically inserting any additional bells and whistles you can recall. As I've said elsewhere, exhaustively complete (long) answers usually score better than brief ones so don't be stingy with your ink. Imagine you are wringing every drop of knowledge from your sponge-like brain. Push yourself hard but also make sure you are managing your time so that you can finish. (Again, most essay exams give you instructions as to how you should allocate your time during the test period. *Follow them!*)

Remember also that you are best served by using short paragraphs in addition to short, crisp sentences. Clarity is a rare pleasure for a grader to encounter.

When you are done with the substantive business of drafting your essays go back and work on presentation, making any corrections and erasures as neatly as possible.

You'll Also Want To "Stick Around" Until The End Of Multiple-Choice Tests

You can always benefit from re-checking answers on multiple choice tests so stick around until the bitter end on those kinds of exams also.

By the way, I hate when people say "don't second-guess yourself on multiple-choice exams because your first answer is usually right." It's not very helpful to advise students to surrender their powers of logic in reviewing their answers. Sure, there is a decent chance that your subconscious mind may have snagged the right answer on the first pass. But, again, if you don't check your work you are susceptible to falling for the **invitingly easy but wrong answer**–a common ploy used by professors on tests.

A better way to think about tough multiple choice questions is to consider whether your answer seems **unambiguously correct**. Fair, well-designed multiple-choice tests require you to complete your analysis and to provide the *right* answer, not just the "best" answer.

If you know the materials well and something bothers you about your answer–if it seems like merely a *decent* answer as opposed to the right answer–step back and reconsider the whole damned question. You may be misinterpreting what is being asked or otherwise missing the point, which is why it feels like you're trying to jam a square peg into a round hole.

Unless the question specifically asks you only for "the best" answer, multiple choice tests are supposed to be about precision and certainty. (Same thing goes for those "draw a line between the words that go together" questions, which are just another version of the multiple choice format.)

If, in the end, you are still feeling even partially stumped–*then* go with your first hunch as the answer.

Chapter VII

"Gettin' Testy Wit It": Curing Test Anxiety And Laughing In The Face Of Death

Key Points

1. Accept control and don't let tests just happen to you.

2. Don't gorge or starve before tests, and walk briskly to class.

3. Make up your own test questions.

4. Target the tough material and drill, drill, drill.

5. Don't hesitate to review your notes right up until the last minute.

6. Study the professor's library test file.

7. Seek out text-specific study aids and online drills.

8. Let your subconscious mind go to work on tests.

9. Don't cherry-pick test questions.

10. Use all time allotted on exams and quizzes.

You can learn to write well, which is good news, because you **must** *learn to write well.* — **G.F.**

Chapter VIII

As The Phrase Turns: Writing Your Way To The Top

A Quick Writing Tune-Up

There are a few simple ways to improve any written assignment beyond your professor's wildest dreams:

1. **Schedule Rewrites.** Before any paper will be good enough to bear your name you will need to rewrite it. Start written assignments early to leave plenty of time for rewriting. Set three progressive deadlines: (i) for completing research, (ii) for completing a first draft, and (iii) for revising and rewriting your first draft.

2. **Read It Aloud.** Never turn in a written assignment without first having read it aloud. Quietly proofreading your papers often fails to eliminate mistakes because your mind tends to see what you had *intended* to write, regardless of what you actually typed. Reading your work aloud will allow you to catch everything from grammatical errors to more subtle flaws in sentence construction and diction.

3. **The Friend Test.** Ideally, you can convince a friend to read

over your paper as well – maybe in exchange for help from you. This is not always possible but it's a great technique. A brilliant teacher taught me the following rule to write by: **Good writing makes the reader feel smart.** Likewise, bad writing can make the reader feel stupid. If a friend with no clue about your subject matter can follow the flow of your paper from paragraph to paragraph, you have done something right.

4. **Good writing is clear, concise and not overburdened with adjectives.** Professors are most impressed with clarity in an essay. They loathe long sentences crammed with flowery phrasing (which usually suggests that you have less, not more, to say). Short sentences and short paragraphs win the day because they are more inviting to read and easier to process. Again, make sure you apply this short and sweet style to your essay exams as well.

5. **Practice Editing.** If you want to learn to see things through your professor's eyes take a whack at editing other students' papers. This will probably be painful, either because they suck so much … or because you realize you have a lot of work to do to get up to par. In any case, be gentle but constructive in offering criticism (and thick-skinned in accepting it).

6. **Use Fresh Eyes.** Arrange your schedule so that you can take *at least* a one-day break before your final rewrite. That way you can attack the document with fresh eyes. Delaying your final polish in this manner will catch all kinds of teensy imperfections and take your gleaming masterpiece to the next level.

7. **I won't remind you to use spell-check because, after all, you aren't a total moron.** This also assumes you are using a word-processor since you aren't some kind of stone-age freak.

8. **Hit the Lab!** Your college may have a writing lab (or whatever

they may call it) with advisors and tutors specially trained to help you improve your papers. *Use these resources.* Let these people read your essays and give you feedback. Why? *Because you will get a better grade.* The writing lab will also have pamphlets or books that provide you with excellent guidelines to turning in winning essays and other written assignments. It is highly unlikely that you learned everything worth knowing about writing college-level papers in high school. Find out where you stand by checking out the writing lab.

9. **Got any Essays on File?** College professors prefer to see papers written according to certain rules and conventions, which the writing lab can help you master. Maybe you can take that to the next level. Remember the "old test file" strategy? It may be the case your professor also keeps a file of student essays that they consider to be exemplary. Or they might be able to suggest other resources to assist you in turning in the kind of work product that really lights their fire. Every professor is going to have slightly different expectations, hang-ups, and pet peeves, so it is useful to try to tailor your efforts to their particular way of thinking. (Get used to this fact about your "bosses"—it's the way of the world.)

10. **Play the Game.** Recognize also that professors grade subjectively. They are human beings who are likely to be influenced by factors that should not necessarily be relevant to whether you score well or not. One such factor is **presentation**. That is why your papers must always be prepared on a computer—as well as error-free and printer-fresh. Right-justifying your text also makes your paper look more pleasing to the eye. Maybe you can even throw in some tasteful computer graphics on your cover page or some other bit of pizzazz (use your best judgment). I took this to a whole other level when I was in college, creating elaborate cover pages which, at best, thrilled my instructors and, at worst, did no harm. Look, you are always going to be graded based on how your papers compare to those

of your classmates. By simply turning in a beautiful-*looking* essay you are taking the opportunity to say: *Hey Professor! I enjoy your class and I have real enthusiasm for the subject matter. In fact, I'm just the kind of bright-eyed, bushy tailed student that got you excited about teaching in the first place! So if you were planning on giving out some A's, why not* **me**?

When writing papers, just **think** *first, long and hard, and then organize your thoughts. At this stage, you don't even have to write anything down. In college, I did some of my best writing in the shower, and I still do. You'll find you can actually compose large portions of essays in your head. The general structure may come to you, along with some specific phrases as well. Then, when you do sit down to write a draft you'll find your thoughts will flow out in a rush, much like a dam breaking.* —**C.E.**

Use Your Computer Screen As A Painter Uses A Canvas

Computers have had a radical effect on creativity in writing of all kinds. The ability to cut, paste and otherwise manipulate text has made writing easier on many levels.

A great way to plow through writer's block, or just kick-start the writing process when faced with writing a paper, is to first type up a few general concepts that you plan to address. Over time, you will refine these concepts into topic sentences, perhaps adding or deleting concepts as you proceed.

As you scroll down your screen, notice that you now have a list of topic areas with room under each for secondary ideas. You can then begin to brainstorm these ideas, referencing your research and whatever else comes to mind. Later, you can refine these ideas into crisp sentences as you see fit.

The beauty of using a computer is that your paper becomes like a canvas would be to an artist–free of the requirements of having to proceed in a linear manner or in any particular order. Should the artist wish to work on a portrait's nose and then switch emphasis completely, adding a few brush strokes to the hair or mouth, that's certainly possible. Like an artist's canvas, a computer monitor also accommodates and even encourages this kind of flexibility and skipping around. Indeed, this method of creation is far more in keeping with the random way the mind generates ideas. (Contrast this to the way an old-fashioned typewriter tends to constrain the writer to draft a document in order, from beginning to end.)

The art of writing on a computer.

You can work on the first paragraph, work on the bare bones of an unrefined concept in the middle, put the finishing touches on the conclusion, rehash the title – whatever comes into your mind.

With such an array of things to work on at your fingertips you will find it is all but impossible to experience writer's block.

Backing up your computer files is mission-critical. There are several ways to do it, and all are easy and inexpensive. If you are using Microsoft® Word there is a simple "auto-save" feature (go to "Options" then "Tools" to find it) that will save your data every 5 or 10 minutes as you type papers. For long-term storage (to guard against hard drive crashes) you can simply burn your data on a CD. Or you can invest in one of those data storage units that periodically backs up your whole computer. They are unbelievably cheap these days. Give it to yourself as a high-school graduation gift. These preventive measures, both short-term and long-term, will probably save your skin dozens of times. College is challenging enough without technical difficulties. If you have ever had your computer crash on you then you know that rewriting papers from scratch is absolute hell. —**E.W.**

But & And

By starting sentences with "But" and "And" you will minimize the use of often clunky words and phrases like "However," "Nevertheless" and "Moreover." (Try "But" rather than "However" to start a sentence, and notice how much better it reads.) Those words tend to suck the energy right out of a sentence, draining paragraphs of momentum. The distinguished usage guru Bryan Garner points out that the reason your grammar-school teacher told you not to start a sentence with "And" was because you wrote, "I have a mother. And a father. And a dog." If you can avoid that childhood syndrome you'll find that "And" is pretty handy.

Good writers also use "But" and "And" to kick off topic sentences at the beginning of paragraphs. That way, the transitions between paragraphs are smooth and seamless. But that doesn't mean you can't judiciously use "But" elsewhere in a paragraph. And don't forget "And."

Very Quite Awful Writing

T ry to limit your use of qualifiers like "very," "quite," "somewhat" and "fairly" in your writing. These fluffy, flabby words tend to drain the vitality from your sentences and may add nothing. Compare these two sentences:

Nietzsche was very obsessed with the quite unusual theory of "eternal recurrence."

with ...

Nietzsche was obsessed with the unusual theory of "eternal recurrence."

Doesn't it feel good to dump that useless verbiage?

Qualifiers can also be illogical or redundant. Take for example "quite unique" or "very first."

Should avoidance of qualifiers be considered a hard and fast rule? No. I break it from time to time. It's just a good guideline to keep in mind.

My friends at QED Press have prepared a useful checklist to keep in mind as you prepare your college essays:

"15 Rules for Writing Good"

• Each pronoun agrees with their antecedent.

• Verbs has to agree with their subjects.

• Don't use no double negatives.

• A writer mustn't shift your point of view.

• Don't use a run-on sentence you got to punctuate it.

• Avoid redundancy that is redundant.

• Don't repeatedly reiterate over and over.

• About sentence fragments.

• Don't use commas, which aren't necessary.

• Don't abbrev.

• Check to see if you any words out.

• Eschew esoteric verbiage.

• Computer spell Czechs are imperfect.

• Never use a preposition to end a sentence with.

• Use apostrophe's right.

• Last but not least, lay off clichés.

Note also that while there is a time and a place for colloquial or informal English (like when I wrote this book, for example). But in general, play it straight and don't get too cute in formal college writing.

Silver-Tongued Bastards

I think we've established that life simply isn't fair. Students who know a few study tricks will soak up all the A's. Similarly, in the professional world, those who are skilled writers are categorized as "management material"—regardless of whether these bullsh*tters are actually hard-working or competent. What can I tell you? Don't hate the playa, hate the game.

Part of becoming an effective communicator is continually expanding your repertoire of language. This is not difficult to do. My father used to say that "once you look up a new word it becomes yours." (He's not dead or anything. He just hasn't said it lately.)

Early in my education, I got into the habit of jotting down interesting words I might run across. To this day, if I really like a word (or a phrase), I post it on the fridge or on my computer monitor, along with its definition and an example of how to use it. If you can pick up a couple of words a month they start to add up.

Those Word-a-Day calendars are also kind of cool. But you have to find one that has some vocabulary you might actually use—not just a bunch of crusty old words that haven't been uttered since the Dark Ages.

Of course, the best way to become a more effective writer and a more compelling speaker is to read voraciously, as a lifetime hobby—not just because someone is making you. Relatively few students, even at the college level, make a practice of reading for pleasure. What you read about on your own can be at least as beneficial as what you are assigned in class. Take your education into your own hands and grab a book! And don't try to tell me you don't have time—*especially* if you can make time to watch the tube.

Chapter VIII

As The Phrase Turns: Writing Your Way To The Top

Key Points

1. Tune up your essays.

2. Use your computer to brainstorm essay material.

3. Avoid clunky phrasing.

4. Habitually improve your vocabulary.

Time isn't just money – it's life itself. Waste enough of it and you'll also lose a piece of yourself. —**G.F.**

Chapter IX

Time Management: The Cornerstone Of Success (And Not As Boring A Topic As You Might Imagine)

Schedule Schmedule, Fudge It With "A Budget"

You've heard it before, *"Time management is critical in college… You must schedule carefully so that the 86,400 seconds in each day don't slip through your fingers like sands through the hourglass, blah, blah, blah…"* Well, take heart because I'm not about to make you suffer through a hypothetical series of pages out of somebody's daily calendar, with 47 minutes set aside for lunch, 21 minutes for folding the laundry and 2 minutes for flossing.

Let me break it down for you:

1. Remember, the main reasons students bite the dust in college are (a) poor study skills and (b) *not spending enough time studying.*

2. The heart of your schedule is already planned for you since your classes meet at set times. Your work schedule and other such obligations would also be essentially pre-scheduled.

3. Do your reading assignments and other class-oriented tasks in the order indicated in your class syllabus to avoid cramming. Your professor is *telling* you how and when to study based on a sensible assessment of how much material you are being asked to master! What happens if you don't follow the professor's recommendations? Maybe nothing – at least not yet. But even if you don't get penalized right away for failing to complete a reading assignment before the next class, you have missed a deadline. This will have a ripple effect. Now you find yourself going to the next class at a severe disadvantage because you may only grasp 50% (or less) of what is being taught. Pretty soon you can't tell your behind from a hole in the wall. Why put yourself through that? Simply complete assignments in the manner the instructor suggests. You will save time and avoid the stress of having to tackle a monstrous work load down the road. One thing's for sure – the amount of work won't get any smaller if you delay. Waiting around instead of tackling your work on schedule only means the information will get harder to cram into your mental databank as time passes.

4. In general, **budget** two hours of study time for each hour of class so you can absorb the information in digestible portions and increase memory retention. (That gives you at least a couple of days to get in your 1-to-2 ratio of study hours until the class meets again since college classes don't usually meet daily.) Thus, while I use the term "schedule" I want you to think in terms of "budgeting" your time so that – whatever happens schedule-wise during the course of your day – you meet your commitment to allocate a set number of hours to studying per day. If you like studying in the morning rather than at night, that's fine with me as long as it gets done.

5. As test time and paper deadlines approach, budget more time over the course of the preceding two or three weeks as appropriate (including time for cumulative class note reviews as discussed later) – but *not* at the expense of your 1-to-2 hour ratio for other classes.

6. That's it! If you do these things, everything else will fall into
its natural place. Specifically, a place that is **secondary** to
studying.

The Kick Ass Study Method In A Nutshell

As I've mentioned, most students think of "studying" as the des-
perate process of keeping up with the wave of information.
These students are constantly operating right on the cusp of their
understanding. Not only are they afraid of the information coming
up–they are even afraid of the information they've already seen.
Why? *Because they can't remember it anymore.*

As you can extrapolate from the last few sections I am asking you
to think of studying as a two-pronged exercise:

1. Stay in front of the waves of information by reading ahead;
and

2. Periodically revisit the information you've seen before.

Come On ... Don't B.S. Yourself

When I make breezy reference to "study hours" what do I mean?
Well, I know what I *don't* mean: wasted, idle hours spent sitting in the library that merely *look* like studying.

Sometimes, when caught up in the excitement of the big dance/
concert/weenie roast, students try to convince themselves that they
have studied plenty of time for the big test when, in fact, they've
basically been jacking around.

What happens when people go to the gym and spend their time
chatting by the water cooler? Nothing. They may be wearing their
weight belt and their spandex thong and their fancy cross-trainers
but if they don't break a sweat and focus they might as well have
stayed home. Same thing goes for you if you fake it at the library

because you can't muster the focus and motivation to make something happen.

So what do you do? You change the way you think about studying, maintaining intensity and efficient use of your time.

I call it…

"Punching In"

To study successfully you must train yourself to do a certain amount of **real work** in a **disciplined manner** within a **fixed time frame**.

Most people can maintain real intensity for about thirty minutes without interruption, at which time they would benefit from a five-minute break before resuming.

When you sit down to study, I urge that you think of it literally as "punching in" at work. My students purchase a small clock or stopwatch with a discreet alarm and go to work in small chunks of time. They set mini-goals for themselves so that they hit targets over the course of the study session. At the end of each half-hour study block they decide whether they are in "the zone" or whether they need their five-minute break. If they want to keep going they give themselves permission to put in another 10 minutes or so, which they also time. The result is that two hours spent studying in this manner can be far more effective than two hours spent sitting aimlessly, hoping for disciplined study to take hold of you.

Look, a stopwatch is just a tool. Ultimately you are going to have to suck it up and motivate *yourself*. You have to have sufficient focus on your *long-term goals* to get fired up for each night of study (much easier when you also have the satisfaction of knowing you are a finely tuned and efficient studying machine).

"Punching in" is a highly effective time management method, especially for students who tend to procrastinate, or those who find it motivating to be highly conscious of the passage of time.

Your time is precious and fleeting.[1] And time is the great equalizer since we all have the same amount in the course of a day, no matter our age or job or anything else.

So remember, kids: ***make time your bitch***.

Power Breaks

I've talked about the importance of taking periodic five-minute breaks. Make the most of this time by taking a minute to go outside and take a few deep breaths of fresh air. It also helps to eat a couple of slices of fresh fruit to give you just a bit of easily digested fuel every hour or so.

Many people around the world swear by a few simple Yoga poses to boost their energy in just a couple of minutes. These poses were developed over thousands of years and work their effects on the body with great speed and efficiency. Yoga also helps you to relax so that you can enjoy the process of success more and take the edge off of your stress.

You might enjoy taking a Yoga class (unless you're self-conscious about your feet or something). Or, you can simply do a little light stretching.

Here's a really good all-purpose stretch: lie down on your back and rest your lower legs on a chair; your legs should be together and your thighs parallel with the legs of the chair so that you get maximum decompression of your spine. *Feels so good.* And it eases fatigue by easing blood flow to the brain for an all-around good use of your break.

Oh yeah, and don't forget to pee.

Your Gigantor Calendar

Go buy yourself one of those giant desk blotter calendars, but don't put it on your desk – instead put it on your wall. (I am *not*, by the way, talking about an erasable white board calendar that requires you to fill in all the numbers every month. We both know those are a pain in the ass, and they smear too easily. It's also better to have the ability to preserve what you've written and to review multiple months, which you can't do if you use a white board you have to erase every month.)

On the first day your professor will make some introductory remarks explaining the manner in which the class will be graded (for example, three tests worth 20% each and a series of quizzes worth a total of 40%). You will also receive a class syllabus with all kinds of exam dates, review session times, paper deadlines and the like. As soon as humanly convenient go home and transfer this information onto your big-ass calendar. It'll only take you about five minutes a class so don't whine. You're better than that.

The idea is to make your schedule seem less like a series of abstract dates and more like a giant map of a journey. Time itself will take on a dimensionality that will better allow you to control it and use it to your advantage. You will always have a constant reminder of your upcoming academic challenges, and your future will seem to "come alive" before it happens. (This is also yet another way to get you to list your goals, which by now you've realized is some kind of psychotic crusade for me.)

You should also pick up an official university calendar and transfer key dates on to your Jumbotron version of your life, such as the last day you can drop a class, the first day of spring break, and other helpful info. Remember to get performing arts and sports schedules if you also want to keep up with those events.

Now then, doesn't it feel good to know what's going on? What a relief not to have to worry about things sneaking up behind you and whacking you on the head.

When you've got this GINORMOUS poster thingy on your wall, continually priming you for crunch times and deadlines, you are miles ahead of those students burying their heads in the sand about their time-sensitive obligations. Hey, somebody's got to make C's.

Enter The Technology Dragon

Not all of my scheduling tactics rely on such retro tools as paper calendars and old-fashioned writing implements. I firmly believe students should rely on a personal data assistant (PDA) such as one of the increasingly inexpensive line of Palm Pilot® devices. Sure, there are fancier models[2] but a basic device that serves as a calendar/alarm, an address book and a calculator will do the job—just so long as you can synch up to a computer and back up your data (the single biggest advantage over an easily lost paper version of your life).

These little technological marvels help make daily scheduling a natural and even vaguely enjoyable part of life.

My favorite feature of the Palm devices (though I hated it passionately before mastering it with a little practice) is the stylus-driven "graffiti" function. And if you download a program like Doodle-Bug, you can actually use the stylus to jot information on the graphical interface screen the same way you would write on a sticky note, which is super-convenient.

Write everything in your PDA calendar from test dates to hot dates, along with all the stuff on your humongous wall calendar. In other words, make your PDA your portable office. You will experience a feeling of security and liberation when you use this device, freeing your mind of mental lint and clutter. Equally important, PDA's are now a staple of business life, so there is a good chance you will be called upon to use one after college.

Kill Your Television

If you're like me, you enjoy television more than you care to admit. As we all know, the bulk of T.V. shows are like greasy, syrupy junk food for the mind. Watching them will do nothing but waste your time. **Contrary to popular belief, watching television is not relaxation.** Because of the passive, sedentary nature of the activity it can actually induce enormous stress and depression.

Now doesn't that feel better?

But let's say you can't live without reruns of Friends, or maybe Judge Judy is your guilty pleasure. Perhaps you like to watch the evening news. Whatever the case, I urge you to *schedule the amount of television you watch each month.* Buy a subscription to T.V. Guide if it will help you to decide what and when you will watch.

Also, personal video recorders (TiVO® is but one such product) have revolutionized television viewing by making it incredibly efficient to record shows and skip commercials.[3]

My suggestion would be that you watch no more than

seven hours a week of T.V., including the weekends. Again, make it a treat to watch your favorite show. If you really want to escape the sin box, just don't get cable…

Okay, you can stop laughing now. But the temptation to waste large chunks of time "cruising" the endless array of channels with the remote can be too hard to resist. (By the way, Playstation® counts as T.V.-watching for these purposes. Play computer games without defined limits at your peril.) Needless to say, not having a T.V. of your own would be the wisest of all courses during your college years since no good can come of on-demand boob-tube access. Or at least consider unplugging the damned thing and stuffing it in your closet during exams.

In short, don't just take the T.V. drug as a way to escape your responsibilities. **If you don't believe T.V. is like an addictive drug, try shutting it off for a week.** The most successful people have substantially moderated or completely eliminated their use of television. Ask any successful person and you will see for yourself.

Okay, if you *really* like television (or film), why not study it? Consider working in the media or entertainment industry.

Regardless, you should seek to become "filmically" literate. Your library may have classic titles available for student viewing. Great films are just as important in your cultural education as great books. You might want to ask your English professor for a list of his or her suggestions, some of which may complement your classes or suggest a topic for a term paper.

Heaving The All-Nighter: A Misguided Odyssey Into The Wee Hours

Sleep deprivation is a common form of torture. Its effects are brutal, both mentally and physically. Whenever you deny yourself one of your most basic needs – whether it be food, water, oxygen or sleep – you aren't doing yourself any favors. Therefore…

Plan, plan, plan so you never place yourself in a position to have to heave an all-nighter. You need at least a few hours of sleep before a test, and preferably the normal seven or eight. This applies whether you think you "feel" tired or not. A sleep deficit *will* undermine your performance, okay? It affects your memory and any number of other cognitive functions.

If you find yourself having to write a paper the night before it's due, you're just not being good to yourself. Moreover, the law of diminishing returns comes into play at around 1 A.M., and you become much less productive as the night drags on. In all likelihood, the assignment you turn in will be nowhere near as good as the one you might have written at a reasonable hour. There is simply no substitute for consistent, daily preparation–and no reason to stay up all night if you punch in every day for work and put in your budgeted hours.

As a rule, you should be in bed by midnight at the latest. If you're a sleep-deprived zombie, you won't benefit much from your morning classes. Get organized and get to sleep.

By the way, artificial stimulants, like coffee, cola drinks and caffeine pills, will thoroughly drain you of energy after a few hours.[4] More importantly, they will ruin your health and make you more susceptible to illness.

I tried some No-Doz® once. They gave me a terrible stomach-ache, like chronic constipation. The worst thing was that I actually slept through the French test I had stayed up most of the night studying for in the first place. Apparently, too much caffeine can make you sleep through an incredibly loud, jangling alarm. When you finally do pass out, you sleep like the dead. Fortunately, I groveled pitifully and the professor let me take the test in his office after everyone else had finished. —**L.L.**

If you must occasionally stay up late (and you will), build up endurance naturally through exercise and good nutrition. Don't become reliant on drugs like caffeine, which can wreak havoc on your system.

Chapter IX

Time Management: The Cornerstone Of Success (And Not As Boring A Topic As You Might Imagine)

Key Points

1. Satisfy your study budget and everything else will fall into place.

2. Make time to stay ahead, take time to review continuously.

3. "Punch in" to make study time count.

4. Use power breaks to keep sharp.

5. Make your schedule "come alive" with a giant calendar.

6. Invest in a PDA and back it up.

7. Don't take the T.V. drug to escape your responsibilities.

8. All-nighters are unnecessary and masochistic.

Chapter IX Notes

1. If you learn one bit of Latin let it be *tempus fugit*, or "time flies."

2. The top-of-the-line Palm-powered treo 650 PDA combines phone, web, email and camera functionalities in addition to the standard calendar/address book/calculator/alarm functions. Soon this type of product will become entry-level and the snazzier models will feature video capabilities and GPS positioning. They may even be able to make you a tuna sandwich. But for now, you can start with something much more basic and inexpensive.

3. Definitely avoid commercials at night, since they bombard you with images of fattening junk food. Like Pavlov's dogs, we race to the vending machines for some sticky nougat goodness or call in for a tire-sized pizza with cheese-injected crust.

4. By the way, you should also avoid sleeping pills, which tend to make you dull-witted the next morning. They can also be highly addictive.

Your memory is a lot better than it even needs to be to make straight A's. It's just a matter of switching it on. — **G.F.**

Chapter X

Congratulations: You've Got A Kick Ass Memory

You Never Forget A Face...
Or Anything Else For That Matter

Your memory is perfect. The trick is learning to move short-term memories into your long-term memory bank. I like to remind students about a bizarre incident that occurred some 25 years ago in which a woman awoke to find her husband talking in his sleep – in a foreign tongue of some kind. The odd thing was that the man had no foreign language skills. Fortunately, his wife had the presence of mind to record her husband's lengthy nocturnal ramblings. It was later determined that the man was speaking perfect, unaccented Russian. It seems that at some point in his life he had been within earshot of two people having a mundane conversation in Russian. For whatever reason, his brain had absorbed this information and randomly accessed it in his sleep, causing him to recite the conversation perfectly. Similarly astonishing results can be obtained through hypnosis.

Gee, I wonder if your memory is good enough to get you through your next Geography test. *Ya think?*

And For My Next Trick...

How would you like to increase your memory power so that you could remember lecture material 75% better? How would you like to fly through the air like a bird? How would you like to disappear and reappear simply by uttering one secret word?

What am I, a magician? I can help you with the memory thing, but the rest you'll have to figure out for yourself.

Lots of magic inside this book.

As a matter of fact, dramatic increases in your memory power are possible, *yes, even without magic.* Nonetheless, such sudden memory power may seem like magic.

To paraphrase the great science-fiction author H.G. Wells, *the science of the future is indistinguishable from the magic of today.* Indeed, science has only recently begun to explain the inner workings of your memory – and how you can turn your mind into an mp3 play-er, capable of recording vast quantities of data. Again, the key is learning to pass information from your short-term memory to your long-term memory. All the memory techniques in this chapter will teach you how to flip this switch.

Boosting your memory power in regard to lecture material in-volves making a surprisingly small sacrifice at the end of each class lecture. Here's how it works:

(1) When the bell rings, do *not* think of it as the end of class. In-stead, think of it as the start of your own personal five-minute mini-class. Rather than stampeding out of the classroom with the rest of the herd, **quietly review what you have just written during the course of the lecture**, adding mate-rial if necessary. This should take you about five minutes. In-credibly, this simple procedure alone will more than *triple* your ability to remember the lecture material. Research has shown that this makes the information "sticky" and far less likely to slip your mind.

(2) You'll notice a definite difference in your memory retention when you review your notes a couple of weeks later. The reason I say "a couple of weeks later" is because you should also **review your cumulative notes for each of your classes every two or three weeks**. This is *sooooo* important! Please do it! It'll take you no more than an hour or two, even toward the end of the semester. Let your notes be a familiar, calming friend – not a disorienting and alarming enemy. There is nothing more frus-trating than not being able to remember or understand what you were trying to memorialize in your notes. **Go ahead and budget those periodic note review sessions into your test preparation time.** I don't want you to be reviewing old notes at the expense of your next reading assignment. (By the way, note review is an ideal task for those times when you have a few minutes here and there since it doesn't absolutely require sustained attention to accomplish. People are always

telling you to make sure and use those little slivers of time to study. But not every type of study is conducive to being done in quick, scattered bursts.)

(3) To further cement facts and figures in your mind, **briefly summarize your notes in written form starting at least one week before your exams**. Writing down information[1] has been shown to be an unparalleled tool for memorization but please make sure (a) that you concentrate on the material as you summarize and write it down so that it doesn't become mindless copying, and (b) that you have budgeted plenty of time for this exercise. The beauty of this technique is that you will also be creating great review materials for use a couple of nights before the test.

(4) To return full circle to the way you got the information in the first place, read your final collection of summary notes **out loud**. This loads the information into your mind yet another way.[2] As you can see, we've now permitted your memory to process the information in a number of different ways for maximum retention and recall. By test time your memory won't even be street legal.

Hear me now and remember me later, these memory tricks work far better than a magic charm when it comes to cementing information in your mind.

The Raunch Factor In Memory Recall

I'm sure you've used **mnemonics** to remember things in the past. Music students, for example, are very familiar with the mnemonic, "Every Good Boy Does Fine" to remember the progression of notes E, G, B, D & F that make up the lines in a treble clef. Mnemonics are highly useful devices because they help you to recall items in a list and, if necessary, in their proper order.

Whether you are making up mnemonics, or drawing diagrams or pictures to aid memorization, think *outrageous*. Create the raunchiest, filthiest mnemonics you can imagine. Embarrass and shock yourself when you create memory aids (or at least make them memorably silly).

The idea, of course, is to permanently burn these phrases and lists into your consciousness so that you can recall them easily. Just be ready to explain to your professors why you blush so much during tests.

No-Card Flash Cards

In theory, flash-cards are a neat idea for memorizing definitions and other smaller chunks of information. But making cards takes time and can quickly become a pain in the ass if you are dealing with a lot of concepts. Pretty soon it becomes more about whether you should put a certain piece of information on one card or two cards, whether you should buy bigger or smaller cards, or use differently colored cards, and so on. My advice is not to get too cutesy when you study. ***Never let the study method tail wag the study dog.***

A better method is to go through your notes and **highlight key terms** you will be called upon to parrot on your exams. If you want to conduct a memory drill, skim through your notes and let your eyes fix upon the highlighted terms. At the same time, cover up the non-highlighted material, filling in any definitions and related information on your own to check your recall. If you need to peek a little at the answers at first, that's okay. Don't panic. A little repetition and the information will begin to gel in your mind.

Remember your awesome inkTank™ erasable highlighter? Pull out the eraser end and, as you cement information, you can erase your highlighting. (If you were using actual flashcards, you would simply set the cards aside as you memorized them. This accomplishes the same thing.)

Chapter X

Congratulations: You've Got A Kick Ass Memory

Key Points

1. Use the Kick Ass memory techniques to increase your retention by 75% or better.

2. The raunch factor can help your recall of handy mnemonics.

3. Save time and drill more with no-card flash cards.

Chapter X Notes

1. Typing may also work for some students but writing is a proven memorization method. A lot of students like to type their notes on laptops, which has its advantages. My own sense, however, is that the information seems to stick better if you physically write it down. But hey, if you can type a mile a second and that works for you I ain't mad atcha.

2. Some students have also had success recording lectures (with their instructor's permission) and listening to them later. In theory, it would always be helpful to hear something twice or to revisit material weeks or months later. My problem with this is that it takes a long-assed time to listen to a lecture again. Your studying could soon become dominated by listening to your godforsaken tapes – and that is not a good idea. The other methods I've described are far more efficient. Sure, if you have a long commute and you have to drive I think listening to recorded lectures would be a decent use of your time. But I would much rather you have a short commute and use the time you save to study your notes.

God helps those who help themselves. Counselors help those who make an appointment. — **G.F.**

Chapter XI

Calling Out The Big Guns: Your Personal Success Team

In College Everyone Can Hear You Scream

You are not in this thing alone. You can't swing a cat without hitting a helpful, well-intentioned member of your campus community. They care about you. They have made education their lives. You should thank heaven for these people every day.

These members of the faculty and staff will be all-too-eager to serve as members of your own personal brain trust. Over time you will assemble your own success team, building key relationships that will make your life approximately 37% easier.

But you must call out to them for help or nobody will hear you.

Campus Resources: Not Just There For Decoration

Here's something else you'll want to post on your wall next to your behemoth of a calendar: **an official map of your college campus**. You can usually find one at the admissions center or the campus bookstore.

Bust out a yellow highlighter and mark the following campus resource centers on your handy-dandy map:

1.   Freshman Services Center

Freshman-centric resources to cover your every question about your college. If your college has a freshman or summer orientation program these folks will be sponsoring it. Practically everything they'll discuss is valuable information, from class registration to dorm life to your school's special traditions... Imagine an uninterrupted stream of pearls of wisdom dripping out of their mouths and try to scoop them all up. And remember: What may sound unimportant today may be tomorrow's solid gold advice or information.

2.   Academic Skills Center/Tutoring Center/Writing Lab

I don't care how well you did in high school, check out these resources and use them.

3.   General Health Center

You'll probably need access to a doctor on campus sooner or later. It's a good idea to get an annual check-up here since many students manage to lose touch with their family doctor when they go off to school.

4.   Mental Health/Counseling Center

Major life changes, such as personal tragedies or the stress associated with starting college, can induce bouts of depression or other mental health challenges. If you ever feel persistently down or unmotivated, or if you are spending more time than normal in bed (or otherwise feeling or acting in a manner that concerns you) you may be experiencing a problem best left to the experts. If someone needs to explore relationship or addiction issues this is also the place to do that. The professionals at your college can discreetly and confidentially assess your situation so you can be in optimal mental shape for college and beyond. Don't let a perfectly treatable problem affect your success in life just because you may feel a little uncomfortable about discussing it. Don't wait around letting personal damage pile up, passively hoping things will improve on their own. The sooner you deal with your concerns the sooner you can put them behind you. You will feel enormous relief after speaking with a caring, knowledgeable person who has heard it all before. (Depending on the situation, you may also wish to draw upon your family for strength and insight during times of difficulty.)

5. Cultural Centers: African American, Asian American, Latino, etc.

Many students find these cultural resources to be beneficial and enriching, regardless of their own ethnic background. These centers are often the sponsors of some of the best campus events and activities.

6. Campus Activities Center/Student Union

Often the nerve center of student government; may feature office space for administrators and other advisors who work closely with students. May also feature a food court and serve as a box office for campus events.

7. Career/Placement Center

There may be more than one career center at your college or university in order to provide specialized career advice and contact information depending on whether you are an engineer, liberal arts major or pre-med, for example. You must visit this center to take the full battery of aptitude tests they have available to help you explore, rethink and narrow your future career choices.

8. Financial Aid Center

It's your birthday! It's your birthday! They're gonna fund you like it's your birthday! ... The Financial Aid Center is always a good source of scholarship information, both for generally available federal or state grants, as well as for those specifically provided for students at your college. (Various departmental headquarters and Deans' offices around campus may also be fruitful avenues to pursue, both for scholarships and for academic prizes and contests that offer cash awards.)

9. Recreation/Exercise Center

Chances are, this is the most efficient and cost-effective place for you to grab a workout and a shower.

10. International Center

Often serves as both a resource clearinghouse for international students as well as a place to obtain information regarding study abroad opportunities and partnerships your college may maintain with foreign centers of higher education.

Plan for a semester abroad in your sophomore year. (Unless you're a language or international studies major that's long enough to have a meaningful experience without throwing you off your degree track.) Nothing will happen on campus that semester, either academically or socially, that can begin to compare to that trip. And you'll never again be as free to take it. As you get further along in college, study abroad gets harder to schedule. You're worried about making all your graduation requirements in four years, you're in a relationship, money is tight, etc., etc. —**P.L.**

11. Center for Students with Disabilities

Many colleges provide one-stop shopping for students with particular needs. May also serve as a meeting place for campus organizations with disability-friendly agendas.

12. Religious Centers

Many colleges have a Hillel Center, Christian Centers of various denominations, Muslim and Buddhist Centers, and a variety of other resources catering to students interested in the four or five most common religious traditions.[1]

13. Alumnae/Mentor Center

Give them a call and ask what services they might provide for currently enrolled students. Career mentoring may be one of their main emphases.

Your campus will not necessarily have all of these resources, but they will have several of them. Be aggressive and learn exactly what is available. *Those resources are there for students like YOU.*

An Academic Counselor Of Your Very Own

An easy way to wreck your life is by not developing a good relationship with an academic counselor. Find out where the academic counselors at your college maintain their offices and schedule an appointment with one early during your first semester.

Academic Counselors: Sure are cute!

Why bother? Mainly for reasons we've already discussed.

1. Academic counselors will ensure that you are on schedule to receive your degree. They will keep you up to date on what classes to take and when to take them.

2. An academic counselor will help you determine whether your proposed course schedule for each semester offers a reasonable, realistic challenge, or whether it will turn you into a ragged basket case.

3. An academic counselor can guide you through the process of skipping certain degree requirements through credit by equivalency tests (and CLEP, as we've discussed), or based upon work you've already performed in high school.

4. An academic counselor can support and advise you in the event of family or health crises that may affect your studies. As referenced earlier, your academic advising office has developed a "safety net" of special rules for handling students' grades in these situations. They may arrange for you to postpone your finals, to take an "incomplete" in one or more classes, or to temporarily withdraw without penalty (so long as you meet all documentation requirements). Uninformed students sometimes compound the effect of personal tragedies by failing to inform their college about a sensitive situation. A strong contact in the academic advising office will allow you to feel more comfortable in dealing with such matters, ensuring that you go through proper channels and generally run all the traps. Specially trained peer advisors may also be assigned by your academic advisor to work with you in an advising or mentoring capacity.

Again, schedule periodic meetings with your academic counselor early each semester and avoid bureaucratic mistakes and hassles that might otherwise haunt you for your entire college career.

Your Financial Aid Solution

It is sometimes financial pressure, and not academic pressure that causes students to crash and burn. College is challenging enough without having to worry about where your next meal will be coming from.

If you are currently receiving financial aid, or if you anticipate a need for it in the future, make a series of appointments with a financial aid counselor when you get to college. Your college or university will assign you a counselor if it hasn't already.

Needless to say, if you are still in high school, use your own school's resources and get up on the financial aid game early. It is especially important to get all the help you can get if you are weighing different financial aid packages that have been offered to you by different colleges. Oftentimes, what, exactly, they are offering you can be difficult to understand. Call those institutions and ask at least five key questions:

1) What kinds of expenses are **not** covered by financial aid?

2) What percentage of the package is in **loans versus grants**?

3) What is expected of me to **maintain** this level of aid?

4) Is this aid **guaranteed** for the length of my degree plan?

5) What are the recommended ways to make up a **shortfall**?

You must understand not only your *present* financial aid situation, but also your *projected* situation for years to come. Only through careful planning will you avoid unpleasant surprises down the road.

Each institution has its own quirky rules for awarding students loans, grants and scholarships. Your financial aid counselor can help you navigate the murky channels of your school's system, to get the most up-to-date information on other types of grants and loans, and to help to assure that your needs are met.

Scholarship applications can be tricky and must be completed to the same standards of neatness and perfection as your essays and other written assignments. Like most everything else in college, you will be in competition with others to win these grants (though it may be surprisingly slim). Have your financial aid counselor review your personal statements and make suggestions. There is definitely a right way to do these things. Don't just wing it.

Remember, your overriding goal must be to develop serious expertise in the business of college financial aid. Depending on your situation, acquiring this kind of knowledge can be every bit as important as your class work. Remember to check out **www.kickass-campus.com** for cutting-edge financial aid solutions.

Go to the best school you can get into, even if you have to borrow a pile of money. That way, you won't be bored for four years. And years from now, your network of brilliant and successful classmates will be worth more as a career (and life) resource. —**P.L.**

Lastly, your financial aid counselor can also help you refine your **budgeting strategies**, and give you a good idea of how much you should be spending each month (stay tuned for more on this).

Making Substitutions

Sometimes, you may not hit it off with somebody who is assigned to work with you as a counselor of some kind. As long as you have reasonably determined that it would be more productive to work with a different individual to address your needs, request a change.

It is your job to assemble the right personnel to serve on your success team. Don't let yourself down because you are worried, for example, about making somebody uncomfortable. You are dealing with professionals. Just be polite and diplomatic about your request and move forward with your life.

Chapter XI

Calling Out The Big Guns: Your Personal Success Team

Key Points

1. Form your own personal brain trust, including an academic advisor and financial aid advisor with whom you meet often.

2. Highlight campus resources on your college map.

Chapter XI Notes

1. By the way, be wary of cults. If you have the slightest doubt about whether an organization is legit, do your research. Some of these outfits prey on young college kids, approaching them through an attractive man or woman. They might invite you to an event, such as a free dinner. Often, they will be vague about the true nature of their little friendship club. *Vague is not good.* Run like the wind. And while we're on the subject of cult-like behavior, if your fraternity wants you to drink 'til you vomit blood, or eat grapes out of someone's behind, do you really want to be a part of that? Surely one of those frats serves fruit in a more appetizing manner and doesn't insist on hazing the crap out of you in the name of brotherhood. Same thing goes for you gals interested in rushing a suitable sorority. Don't let anyone strip you nekked and circle your "problem areas" with a permanent marker. Not nice.

When someone asks, "Who do you think you are?" you're probably doing something pretty badass. Tell them, "I don't have to think about it–I know who I am."—**G.F.**

Chapter XII

Making A Name For Yourself: If You Don't Toot Your Own Horn, Ain't Nobody Gonna Toot It For You

Getting Your Extracurricular On

The time will come when you will want to begin thinking about extracurricular activities. The second semester of freshman year is generally a good time to get involved, assuming you have already built the foundation for a solid G.P.A. Take time out during your first semester to research organizations and activities. Go to your campus activities office or to your dean of students' office to obtain lists and descriptions of student groups at your school (don't just blindly gravitate toward whatever your dormmates seem to be into). Attend a few meetings of the organizations that interest you, and gauge the time commitment membership in each might entail. **Always keep in mind that you are scheduling extracurricular activities around schoolwork, and not the other way around.**

Some people join organizations merely to "pad" their resumes, never intending to do more than the bare minimum required. This attitude will waste your time and that of your fellow members. Your lack of interest and your reluctance to take on responsibility will quickly identify you as "dead weight." Never join an organization unless you feel you can invest both time and emotional energy in the goals of the group. Matter of fact, if you haven't taken on a position of some kind in the group after a year, you are probably a mediocre member.

Ask yourself the following when analyzing your decision to join a campus or other group:

1. How would membership in this organization benefit me? Is it relevant to my career goals? Will I have a reasonable chance to assume responsibility and leadership if I make a strong commitment?

2. Do I actually like the people in the group? Will I have fun? Recognize that this organization will be an important source of opportunities for socializing.

3. Is this organization respected on campus? Does it strive to maintain a diverse membership, or will I meet a bunch of similar people?

Juggle Like A Mo' Fo'

Extracurricular activities should provide valuable experience in leadership and administration. By your in-depth participation you are also demonstrating to prospective employers and graduate schools that you can juggle several responsibilities at once. This is important.

Juggling, after all, is what adulthood is all about: juggling your job, your family, and everything else in your life. In college, you must demonstrate the ability to juggle your grades, your extracurricular activities, any work obligations, your relationships, and all of the other potential responsibilities foisted upon you by college life.

Of course, part of a successful juggling act means knowing when to juggle only six chainsaws rather than seven.

We're all jugglers.

Don't get over-extended trying to build your resume. As important as extracurricular activities are, acing your classes comes first. I tried to cram a part-time job, an honors thesis, and being an officer in three organizations into a schedule that also happened to include a full semester of classes. Anyway, things were really going down the tubes after a couple of months. I visited my college advisor, who urged me to cut back on my responsibilities in a big way. So I reluctantly pared back my hours at the job. While I kept one leadership position, I demoted myself to rank-and-file status in the remaining two groups. My grades shot up and my stress level went way down. Seems like a no-brainer now but when you're caught up in a frenzy of activity, sometimes you need an outside perspective to figure things out. —**M.K.**

Looking Great On Paper: Becoming The "Total Package"

It is always impressive when you demonstrate, by way of the activities listed on your resume, that you have shown committed and extensive interest in a given area. Employers and graduate schools look favorably on individuals who have demonstrated passion for scholarship (first and foremost), interesting experiences (extracurrics and internships) – as well as the traits of a team player (again, extracurrics and internships). In short, they like to see applicants who are the "total package." Why don't we kick around some examples...

Let's say that Marcie (or Joanie or Chachi or whomever) has decided to seek admission to a graduate school to pursue a degree in Spanish. What sorts of extracurricular activities might benefit her as a prospective applicant? *Hmmm...* how about:

Spanish Honor Society, Treasurer (demonstrates scholastic achievement)

Amnesty International, Campus Coordinator (demonstrates political and international awareness)

Semester in Spain (demonstrates maturity and independence; commitment to mastery of Spanish language)

Summer Program in Mexico (in conjunction with the above, reinforces commitment to the study of culture and language)

Student Council Representative (demonstrates leadership and willingness to accept responsibility)

Office Assistant, Mexican Consulate (demonstrates responsibility and experience with relevant population)

You get the idea. Let's look at Phillip, an applicant to law school:

Digital Rights Coalition, Student Liaison (demonstrates political involvement; awareness of cutting-edge legal issues)

Spring Semester Internship, Office of State Representative (great experience in local government)

Summer Internship, Office of Congressman (great experience in federal government; solidifies commitment to mastering political process)

Pre-Law Fraternity, Vice-President (demonstrates exposure to field and commitment to legal profession)

University Daily News, Staff Writer (demonstrates interest in community; writing expertise; communication skills)

Am I making sense? See how interesting and well-rounded these imaginary people sound? Okay, one more ... Penelope is interested in landing a position as a computer analyst at a financial services company:

Penelope's Word-Processing & Resume Service, Proprietor (demonstrates real-world business experience; responsibility and maturity)

Dell Computer Company, Summer Internship (demonstrates exposure to Fortune 500 business entity)

Disabled Students Union, Co-Chair (demonstrates leadership)

Boys & Girls Club Volunteer (demonstrates commitment to community)

Well, that was fun. Anyway, these examples should give you a basis for thinking about how you might shape your own extracurricular life.

What kind of impression will *you* make after four years of College? With determination and hard work you will be able to crow about some academic honors on your resume as well, like making the Dean's List or winning a prize in an essay contest sponsored by the Philosophy Department. That kind of thing.

You need a basic resume, even as a freshman. The kinds of superstar opportunities you will be pursuing will require you to present yourself professionally. Your first step in creating your first resume is to catalog your activities and achievements throughout high school and leading up to college. While you probably won't want to include your experience at Chick-Fil-A® or as part of a lawn mowing crew when you apply to law school four years from now, it's all good when it comes to presenting yourself as a student fresh out of the 12th grade. If you were involved in sports, Scouting, charity events, whatever – document that stuff. Be proud of things you've accomplished and participated in as a young person.

You may not think you have much to put down on your resume right now, or you may think the process is too painful to begin working on as a freshman. Not true. You can do it! The resume process is much simpler than you might think.

As with most things, the key is simply to get started. Pay a visit to your Career Center and request a computerized resume template. Next, just plug in your info. Lastly, ask for some feedback from a career counselor. Congratulations, you're done.

As time passes, you can easily supplement your resume. Soon, you'll have *too much* (your college resume must all fit on one page) and you will actually need to weed things out! By the end of freshman year, you will have a perfectly adequate resume for someone early in their college career. In general, just relax. No one is expecting you to be Vice-President of IBM by sophomore year. At the end of four years, your resume will be a source of confidence and pride. As a bonus, the completion of a resume will do wonders for your focus and motivation.

Take Me To Your Leader

During the course of your four years at college, it is imperative that you aggressively pursue a leadership position in a campus organization. Surveys consistently show that campus leaders become society's leaders. Think employers like that? You bet.

Want To Start Something?

You might also consider the idea of starting an organization yourself. If there is a void to be filled in your school's list of campus activities and organizations, by all means fill it! Just be sure to invest your time and energy in a venture with meaning and substance, *e.g.*, a "Campus Libertarians Club" or an "African-Americans in Journalism" group, rather than "The Fast Food Appreciation Society."

It's cool to be a founder of something valuable. And it shows you have big brass balls (or "chutzpah" if you want to be polite about it).

Snowballing Honors

As a general rule, seek to maintain a reasonably high profile through as many activities as your schedule comfortably allows. This will speed your entry into the circle of students frequently considered for awards, school presentations and other honors. The idea here is not to achieve world domination. It is to secure as many **options** as possible by placing yourself in contention for plum opportunities.

Thus, the more you get involved in the extracurricular life of your institution, the more you will be nominated for honors. You might get an "Outstanding Student" or community service award. If invited to join an honor society, by all means, accept (unless they are organizations that ask you for some kind of fee to join, like the Golden [insert random object here] Society, or Who's Who Among College Doofuses Who Pay to be Mentioned in a Book Nobody Cares About).

You may even be singled out for an academic scholarship or a cash award of some kind. Academic and extracurricular honors tell employers and graduate schools that your peers and professors respect your contributions to the institution. As such, collegiate honors serve as dramatic evidence that you have **"mastered the college system."**

Look, a lot of this college success stuff is a game. It's not bad, it's not good. It is what it is. For example, some colleges have a tendency to give many of the same honors to the same high-profile students. Sometimes these awards snowball and once you get one or two, you tend to be in line for several more. Colleges love to honor their movers and shakers, as well they should.

Again, if you are nominated for an academic accomplishment or for some contribution you have made, make sure you pursue the honor. Sometimes the committee in charge of awarding the honor may require you to fill out a supplementary statement elaborating on your achievements. Do it! Even if you are rejected a few times, you will eventually win something. The more your name is bandied about among students and administrators, the more likely you are to take the brass ring one way or another. Winning an award is always a blast, and it will make a wonderful addition to your resume.

Mamas Don't Let Your Babies Grow Up To Be A-Holes

Another key aspect of your journey into the stratosphere of stellar students is to handle yourself properly. "Handling yourself properly" means being at least as focused on team objectives as on your own personal glory. It means being respectful in the way you offer and accept criticism, and being willing to offer and accept compliments with grace. (Just don't try too hard or come on too strong – people will feel slimed if you are heavy-handed with either praise or self-deprecation. You need only be sincere.) It means having the ability to recognize when someone has a better idea, and getting behind it. Finally, it means always remembering what it was like when you were just starting out as a green freshman, and doing your best to help any new students who come to you for help and advice. Success is pointless if it is completely self-serving. Besides that, it's no fun.

Yes, it is important to receive recognition when it is due. But as a wise man once said, **"It's amazing what you can accomplish when you don't care who gets the credit."** If you approach life from this perspective, things will fall into place on their own. Generosity is far more attractive and productive than pettiness and neediness. Be alert to the impressions you are making through your words and deeds. Don't adopt a small-time mentality by angling for every bit of credit. There is plenty of success out there for everybody.

Don't Have A Credibility Gap

If you commit to do something, for goodness sakes', *do it*. I don't care if you're making promises to professors or peers in a student organization, if you are unreliable you are useless to them. If you can be trusted to do what you say you are worth your weight in gold.

If you don't know whether you can follow through on a task – or if you already know you in advance that you cannot fulfill a promise you are thinking of making – don't sacrifice your solemn word. That's your *reputation* we're talking about. And there is nothing harder to repair than the reputation of a liar.

An unfulfilled promise is a helluva lot worse than a promise never made. (On the other hand, if you're not making promises you could and should make simply out of laziness, that's not so hot either.)

Be A Hero

You don't want to be the type of person who instantly accepts "no" or "I don't know" for an answer. You want to be politely tenacious and pleasantly persistent.

There are innumerable examples of what I mean but let's say, for instance...you call "411" for information in Toledo, Ohio, because you were told that you could contact a particular business there. But the operator tells you there is no business by that name in Toledo. Do you give up? Of course not. First, you get your money's worth by making sure the operator performs the search in the surrounding area. Then you get him to try alternate spellings. If that fails, you try the internet, and then you call the source who gave you the information in the first place.

If this course of action sounds obvious to you, great. Otherwise, you want to incorporate a little of this pit bull instinct into your personality. Latch on to problems and don't let go until you've gotten what you want. Only don't try to draw blood – instead, use your charm and people skills to shake something loose.

To paraphrase Ralph Waldo Emerson, the only difference between a hero and an ordinary person is that the hero tries for five minutes longer. Try to be a hero – even in small ways – every day. You'll find that's the kind of person others respect and want to be around.

Getting Ahead In A Dog-Eat-Dog World
Through Small Acts Of Decency

As I've suggested, there are certain little things you do in life that can set you pleasantly apart from the rest of the pack. Here are a couple of impressive habits that will help you say, *"Hey world, I've got some kick-ass manners and I'm goddamned polite... and don't you forget it!"*

1. **Thank-You Notes: Your Secret Weapon for World Conquest.** Hard to believe, but thank-you notes make an unbelievable impression in the adult world. People just eat them up like little silver dollar-sized blueberry pancakes. In fact, many believe that thank-you notes were entirely responsible for getting George Bush (the elder) elected President. The man carried a box of cards with him everywhere he went on the campaign trail. Immediately following each event, he would jot down a thank-you note to each of the volunteers or hosts who helped out. There are thousands of these things floating around, probably on eBay. One silly reason people don't send thank-you notes is because they don't own basic stationery, and they seem to have no idea how to obtain it. Here's what you do: go to your local Kinko's and order some "correspondence cards" (index-card sized notes) with your full name printed smartly at the top, along with some matching envelopes. That's it! For your purposes, brief thank-you notes should be written to faculty, staff and others for assistance rendered or favors done. Always, always, always do this within 72 hours. (Revenge is a dish best served cold. Gratitude is a dish best served *promptly*.) Besides "thank you," what do you say in a thank-you note? Try this format:

    *   For starters, you can use "Dear" in addressing professors and staff – it's kind of nice and respectful. But you need not do it if you don't feel comfortable. In any case, the recipient is unlikely to think you have a crush on them if that's what your worried about. *Sheesh.*

- Next, express appreciation. ("Thank you for your thoughtful assistance in helping me with my tutoring needs.")

- Next, mention the benefit rendered. ("Jennifer is a terrific Economics tutor with a gift for explaining the material clearly.")

- It may be nice to end by mentioning a future meeting. ("Look forward to updating you on my progress at the Tutoring Center soon.")

- Sign off with the time-tested "Sincerely, [your name here]" or I like to use the simple phrase "Best, Gunnar." (By the way, don't ever use "Best regards" to end a letter if you have never met or at least corresponded with them before–that's very bush league. And unless you are corresponding with Tammy Fae Bakker try not to end with "Yours in the faith…")

2.   **Name Recognition.** Whenever you meet someone you don't see regularly, remind them of your name. It takes a lot of the stress out of these kinds of interactions and, just as important *–they really will remember your name.* It's crucial for you to be known by name in almost any field of endeavor. College is no different.

3.   **Burnishing Your Image with "Clients."** It is instructive to note that certain cab drivers double their tips by *doing more than anyone would ever expect.* They offer their passengers a choice of newspapers. They treat them to cold drinks or fresh fruit. They ask if the temperature in the cab is comfortable, or whether the rider might prefer a particular music or talk radio station. Without being obtrusive, they treat their customers as their guests. These are not grand acts of generosity–just simple acts of humanity. Most likely, you aren't going to college to drive a cab. But you will probably end up in a professional career where you have clients of some kind…and *this*

is the way to treat your clients. Right now, today, your clients include anyone who impacts your college career. Now I'm not suggesting you go raid gift shops and start baking cookies. You need not necessarily think of "gifts" and "tokens" as literal items. It's more a question of maintaining the attitude and respect that your good clients may not expect, but which they do deserve.

Must you do these things? Certainly not! The things that you *must* do in life are very few, indeed.... Eat. Drink. Sleep. Maybe a couple more that escape me right now. But that's about all life really asks of you.

Having said that, if you want to fly first class through life, then, yes, you *must* be sharp enough and motivated enough to do things nobody even expects you to do. And you *must* strive to be that one in ten, or one in a hundred, or one in many thousands, that does things the way they ought to be done.

Handling Conflict: The Art Of Taming Your Animal Instincts

A lot of the issues we are discussing in this chapter deal with your "E.Q." – a term some smarty-pants coined for our "emotional intelligence." Our E.Q. is not only important during those times when we are trying to butter people up. It's also critical when people are ticking us off, or vice versa.

Assuming you don't find yourself in an Ultimate Fighting Championship death match with some guy named "Dozer," chances are that you will experience most conflict in the form of heated conversations. If an emotionally charged verbal exchange is about something important to you, and the outcome could have a major impact on your life, you'd better have a strategy for these situations.

First, let's understand the way in which we are trained by nature to handle conflict in a rational manner: **we aren't**. When we start arguing and our temper flares, we experience a sudden burst of adrenalin. (You've heard this referred to as the "fight or flight" response, common to all animals, including humans.) At this point, the blood drains from our brains and flows into the big muscles in our arms and legs. Thus, our protective instincts actually work *against* our ability to reason calmly. We may not start pummeling the other person right away but we do tend to say things we regret. If we are under pressure to answer questions or accusations, we are more easily confused. We may start making things up or freaking out. What may have started as a healthy dialogue can soon degenerate into a pissing contest. The conversation becomes about "winning" and saying nasty things that wound the other party.

Another problem we experience when we are in this highly adrenilated state is what I call "Sucker's Choice[1]" syndrome. This means your thoughts get so muddled that you mistakenly feel that you have only two behavioral choices, both of which *suck*. For example, when things get hairy in an argument, you convince yourself that you only have two options: (a) "silence" (clamming up and turning your rage inward) or (b) "violence" (exploding in rage and accomplishing nothing).

Another sucker's choice would be: (a) "sugar-coating your concerns and preserving calm" versus (b) "being honest and thus rude." People, people, *pleeeease*. Can we be a little more creative? The truth may hurt but it need not be rude or disrespectful.

When you feel your adrenalin pumping during one of these hardcore chats, dial it back a notch and slow down. Realize that your brain is disengaging and your fiery emotions are taking over. Make a conscious effort to overcome your animalistic responses and focus on what you are trying to achieve. You are probably struggling with some complicated issues that require clear-headed analysis. Only with a cool head and a controlled ego can you come up with a fair solution to a complicated human equation.

Here's the most important point…If you're fixin' to have an important conversation that has the potential to become a knock-down, drag-out affair, try to decide the following on the front-end:

(1) what outcome(s) you want; and

(2) what outcome(s) you don't want.

Ideally, you'll have time, well in advance, to prepare mentally for your momentous chat. I would even consider drafting an outline of your thoughts and perhaps even practicing the process of calmly making your points with a friend. It may actually help you better understand and define your thoughts and feelings if someone plays devil's advocate as you lay out your position.

Chapter XII

Making A Name For Yourself:
If You Don't Toot Your Own Horn,
Ain't Nobody Gonna Toot It For You

Key Points

1. Carefully evaluate extracurricular opportunities.

2. Part of being a good juggler is knowing your limits.

3. Your extracurricular record should reflect depth and commitment.

4. You need a basic resume, even as a freshman.

5. Commit to obtaining a position as a student leader.

6. Handle yourself properly on your way to the top.

Chapter XII Notes

1. They used to call this a "Hobson's choice" but nobody knows what that means anymore so I've just sexed it up a little.

Life isn't fair but what is? In one way or another, we're all playing on an uneven playing field that doesn't favor us. Never hesitate to use your gifts to compensate for the rough spots. — **G.F.**

Chapter XIII

Sucking Up: A Lost Art

People Skilz

For some students, the most intimidating aspect of college life is relating to the faculty and staff. They watch their college's officials from afar, never approaching them for help, or even just to offer a simple "hello."

DID YOU KNOW?
Professors molt twice a semester!

And yet professors, for example, are just like you and me. (Granted, they undergo periodic molting periods and have two spinal columns, but aside from that, they're just regular folks.) They aren't gods. They have families and lives and run-of-the-mill problems with their cars and plumbing.

There are many reasons for you to get to know the people running your institution and grading your performance. Intuitively, you know that a good relationship with your professor will benefit you. You realize that while it won't guarantee you an A, it *will* guarantee you an edge…and little edges here and there are the stuff that A's are made of.

Still, surprisingly few students take steps to build a good rapport with professors and administrators. Some students are too shy, while others don't know what to say. Still others do not want to be seen as "sucking up." **Well, I'm here to tell you that "sucking up" has gotten a bad rap.**

We're basically talking about using your people skills – the same skills that will continue to serve you well in your dealings with employers and colleagues throughout your career. Your conversations with your professors and with other professionals you encounter in college provide valuable opportunities to practice building rapport with leaders in our society.

As long as you have something productive and useful to discuss with your professor, can you help it if he or she will come to take a liking to you? I'm not suggesting that you go out of your way to exchange idle pleasantries with every professor within earshot. But I am saying that every student has an abundance of legitimate questions and concerns they would do well to share with faculty and administration officials. Recognize this and be prepared for situations in which you will have contact with these interesting and influential people.

The Secret Lives Of T.A.'s & Professors

Your T.A. will usually be a professor-in-training hired to assist your professor in teaching and administering a large class. These people are usually graduate students who have distinguished themselves in their fields and who are extremely passionate about the subject matter. The T.A. usually assists the professor in grading papers, answering questions during office hours, and leading discussion and review sections.

Some professors deliver class lectures but leave virtually every other responsibility for running the class to one or more teaching assistants. This is most often true in the case of well-known professors who lecture to hundreds of students.

Most T.A.'s are highly competent, sympathetic individuals. But once or twice during your college career, you will encounter a T.A. on a power trip. Their responses to your questions will drip with condescension, and you will find yourself fighting the urge to slap them into the middle of next semester. Don't sweat it. If your T.A. is a little arrogant, rise above it and realize he is probably just trying to earn your respect by acting "professorish." Whatever you do, try to stay on his good side, if he has one.

In larger classes, it is the T.A. who holds your academic life in the palm of his or her hand. I recall once taking a Government class with about 399 other students. On the first day of class, the professor gave us a breakdown of how she would calculate our grades: 50% would be based on test scores, 20% on a paper we would write at mid-semester, and 30% on our final exam. I made careful note of her last comment regarding grades: *"Your participation in a weekly discussion section led by one of four teaching assistants might also be a factor in borderline cases."*

I enjoyed participating in the T.A.-led discussion sections, which usually degenerated into a no-holds-barred political argument. I always advise students to jump in the fray during discussions because (a) it keeps them attentive, (b) sharpens public speaking skills, and (c) *distinguishes them from the pack.*

It turned out to be a pretty tough class. At the end of the semester, I learned that my tests, my paper, and my final exam had only averaged to an 89–one point short of an A-. Fortunately, I had developed a good rapport with my T.A., who had appreciated my enthusiasm over the course of the semester. I had also taken regular advantage of his office hours. The T.A. agreed that I should be granted an extra point given my contributions to the discussion section. The T.A. tracked down the professor and personally saw to it that the paperwork required to change my grade from a B-plus to an A-minus was submitted that same day.[1]

Don't assume that no one will pay attention to your individual concerns in a large class. If you deserve a better grade than you received, you should speak up for yourself, asking the T.A. to serve as your advocate if that makes sense. (But if you clearly got what you deserved, don't whine or the T.A. might actually take away points. At least he should. It's only fair.)

Don't let large classes get you down. As long as you make a personal connection with your T.A. or your professor, the big class will be tolerable. Some students don't believe that instructors will ever remember them in a class of three to four hundred. This is not true. Pessimistically, a professor in a huge class will remember about 10% of the class, a T.A. about 15%. Ensure that you are among those whose names are remembered! Whenever possible, sit in the front row, where you will easily see and be seen. A class of 400 might as well be a class of twenty from this perspective.

The Care And Feeding Of Faculty Members

As I've alluded, it's a great feeling to walk into an instructor's office and say, "Hello Professor Chung, my name is Gunnar and I'm in your 11 o'clock Astronomy class," and to have him reply, "Yes, of course, I remember you. What can I do for you?"

Okay, so now what? One simple rule should apply to your interactions with faculty members…Hemingway once said that the secret to good writing was having your own "bullsh*t detector." The same applies to productive interactions with faculty. You have no need to bullsh*t anyone.

Be yourself—a conscientious student who is concerned about learning the class material and making a good grade. This is all anyone expects. You don't have to compliment them or mesmerize them or impress them to death. A little honesty goes a long way.

One Friday morning late in the Spring I found myself walking to my 8:00 a.m. Spanish class with half an hour to spare. I must have been coming straight from an all-night party because I had neither text nor homework with me, nor any recollection of where I had been for the last several hours. But at least I was going to get to class early. My professor, Dr. Toledo, was a thirty-year-old Cuban refugee who was as hot-tempered as she was, well, hot. Upon learning that I had blown her class off, I was certain she would chew me up and spit me out like a mushy Cohiba cigar. I had seen her reduce a classmate to tears for a lesser offense. My head hurt, my stomach churned, and my eyes still twitched from the prior evening's activities. I resolved simply to submit to Dr. Toledo's wrath and take my punishment. I snapped off the tip of a tree branch in full bloom and stepped into the converted WWII ROTC barracks that hosted Spanish I. Dr. Toledo looked up as I swayed in the doorway, beckoning me into her chamber. I told her forthrightly that I had stayed out all night, failed to do my assignment, forgot my textbook and was unprepared for her class. I held out the flaming-pink flowering branch and stammered that I had picked the blooms for her in a feeble, awkward attempt to convince her that I did take her class seriously and was genuinely sorry. Dr. Toledo watched me inscrutably, handed me her text and told me to sit down and start studying the day's assignment. She smelled the pretty flowers and laid them gently on her desk. I opened the book and I waited for my classmates to arrive to witness my impending humiliation. Keeping to her habit, Dr. Toledo grilled her students going down each row, left to right. I could predict the exercise I would be called upon to translate by counting the number of students between the

*one reciting and myself. Even so, my eyes would not focus, nor could my brain make sense of all the foreign words in the lengthy passage I knew would fall to me. My time came. Dr. Toledo's eyes burned through mine. She smiled, just barely. And then turned her head and called on the girl sitting next to me to translate the passage. "But you skipped Jay!" the terrified freshman blurted, caught completely off guard, one exercise behind where she needed to be. Dr. Toledo insisted she go forward with the passage and then ripped her apart for her lack of preparation. Moral of the story: Professors will plea bargain from time to time. Just make sure you get your plea in early. — **J.J.***

Cultivating Mentors

Next to a parent, your college professor could be the most influential mentor you will ever have. **Get to know at least two professors well.** (Again, not a bad thing to include in your goals list.) Wait for the right opportunity to switch gears and have an informal conversation with them. Here's an idea: ask them about the range of subjects they teach or what their responsibilities entail. Most people love talking about themselves.

If your organization is hosting a faculty-student breakfast, make sure you invite a couple of professors. If you organize a group or activity, ask a professor to serve as a faculty advisor. While most professors are busy with research and their classroom responsibilities, many will make time to work with you if at all possible. Great professors recognize that part of their mission is to make a personal investment in their students.

Model your instructors, both in their approach to their studies and in the manner in which they have planned, and continue to plan their careers. Take an avid interest in the career path that brought your professor or T.A. to your school. Most instructors will welcome the opportunity to relate their career story and give you advice when appropriate.

Remember that faculty members can serve as powerful references for you when you apply for jobs and graduate programs after college. Many applications for these positions require at least two such references from instructors who know you well.

The Dean Of Your College: A True Player

Deans of colleges are usually distinguished professors appointed by the president of your college or university to handle the administrative decisions and duties in a certain academic area. The dean's responsibilities may extend to hiring, professorial tenure issues, fund-raising and curriculum design.

As you build your reputation as a rising star, both academically and as a student leader, you may have some contact with your Dean. The Dean may ask you to speak at a school event, or to participate in recruitment efforts. These are each great privileges which you should accept if at all possible.

Don't hesitate to speak with the Dean of your college if appropriate. He or she is *your* Dean. Questions or concerns may arise, for example, as you become involved with student government issues. Early in my college career, I made an appointment to see my Dean about the possibility of launching a community service initiative for our college. He was excited about the idea and inspired me to follow through. Later that year, he permitted me to interview him for a class I was taking on leadership skills. Whatever you do, come well prepared!

Follow up your meeting with a brief thank-you note for his or her time, along with an update of any action you might have taken as a result of the interchange. You get the idea.

The next time the Dean needs a student to assist with an important project, your name may spring to mind. As you can well imagine, your Dean can also serve as an impressive reference.

The President: Hail 2 The Chief

Depending on the size of your college or university, the school president may be a familiar person to you. Most presidents of institutions of higher learning, along with other members of the faculty and administration at your school, are some of the most charismatic and interesting people you will meet, regardless of whether you like the decisions they make.

College presidents may appoint student leaders to special standing committees along with important faculty and administration officials. These committees often deal with critical aspects of the functioning of the institution, *e.g.*, student housing, tuition increases, minority recruitment and retention, and financial aid. Membership on such a committee may allow you to have significant impact on the decisions ultimately handed down from the president's office.

Don't let any of this talk about meetings in the president's chambers freak you out. I'm just trying to give you an idea of what your success might look like in a couple of years.

Needless to say, a reference from the President extolling your good works will get you a long, long way.

The Secretary: Large And In Charge

The secretary (or "administrative assistant," as some prefer to be called) sits at the very apex of power, wielding enormous influence in many areas. For example, a secretary often determines whether and when you will be given a slot in someone's schedule. People in key positions are often swayed by their secretaries' opinions. A secretary in your corner may help you snare nominations or honors. If you are on a list of ten people up for a prestigious scholarship and the Dean's secretary offhandedly utters, "You know, that *Sylvia* is certainly a deserving young woman," you're golden.

Always go out of your way to build good rapport with secretaries. While you await an appointment with an official, chat with the secretary and other support staff and make them feel appreciated.

Office workers are not always accorded the proper respect by snobbish students.

The lesson here is not that you should be selectively friendly to certain people of influence, but rather that you be decent to everyone – even those who may not be able to do you a damn bit of good.

There is great power in gestures of kindness. Take responsibility for helping to make your school community a warm and pleasant place to live and work. What goes around comes around in college and in life.

Chapter XIII

Sucking Up: A Lost Art

Key Points

1. You *must* cultivate professors as mentors.

2. Build rapport with *all* members of your college community with whom you come into contact.

Chapter XIII Notes

1. If you are planning to put in for a grade change act as early as possible. Such changes become administratively more difficult to make as time passes.

If you want your dreams to come true, wake up! —**G.F.**

Chapter XIV

Snagging A Good Gig: It's All About Persistence

Major Indecision

You may hear people tell you not to worry if you haven't chosen a major yet.[1] "Let a couple of years pass and wait to see if something leaps out at you." Needless to say, you can fertilize your lawn with this kind of advice and it will grow green, lush and pretty. Yup, it's what we used to call "ca-ca" when I was a kid.

There's nothing wrong with not knowing exactly what your major will be. But you must avoid taking a *laissez faire* approach to any aspect of your life (*laissez faire,* of course, is French for "sitting around on your can and watching the world go by"). Rather, you need to invest a great deal of conscious energy in exploring your aptitudes, interests and dreams. You can't expect your future career to fall out of the sky and bonk you on the head.

Again, I'm not pressuring you so much to choose a major right away. But I am urging you to begin immediately to seek one out. Just hurry up and get your feet wet, and you will see that the water is just fine.

Now then, here's your three-step plan for major/career exploration:

Step One: Test Yourself

Go to your college's career center and arrange to see a counselor. Ask to take the most extensive battery of career aptitude and personality tests available. This is an astonishingly revealing exercise, even for those of you with a fairly clear idea of what your future holds. Aptitude tests have particular usefulness when students have a number of strong and seemingly conflicting interests. It helps to think of "aptitude" tests as "Do What You Love" tests. Maybe you love playing with peoples' minds. That suggests a number of careers. Psychologist? Car dealer? College professor? The world is your oyster. **Testing may also reveal a totally unanticipated career path that may allow you to reconcile several passions.** In general, when you can visualize your exciting future career and identify a corresponding major your enthusiasm for pursuing your education will increase to a fever pitch. As you know, wild-eyed enthusiasm is part of your formula for stellar success. By the way, the Career Center will be able to give you further information on the job search process, and on the specifics of various careers that may interest you.

Step Two: Build Your Rolodex

Arrange to speak with experts in your field(s) of interest. Specifically, seek out mentors who can speak to you in detail about their chosen professions. Such interaction will often answer questions you never even thought of asking. Mentors can be contacted through your career center's mentoring programs, through the alumnae center or through the Yellow Pages. If you are a bit shy about speaking with these folks, this is quite normal, but please *get over it.* You must set aside your shyness and hesitancy to pursue meetings with people who can help put your education into overdrive by connecting you with your potential future. You will be amazed at how receptive most people in the professional world will be to your requests for information. Nothing is more satisfying than serving as a mentor for a student with an attentive ear, a curious mind and solid ambition. It's actually quite flattering. Arrange to visit your mentor at his or her workplace. Depending on the situation, there may be some cool opportunities to attend meetings, events or negotiations, or to see designs or works-in-progress. After a few of these experiences you can really begin to visualize yourself in several potential careers. Your future becomes more tangible as these possibilities begin to crystallize in your mind. This is all about taking an aggressive approach to seeking out a major and a career, and thus demystifying the job search process. As always, you must *take control.*

Step Three: Get a Foothold

Parlay your contacts into relevant experience when you pursue internships or summer work. Your career counselor can also refer you to job listings and other resources in your job search, and help you with interviewing skills. Be prepared to consider working in a volunteer capacity before you gain enough experience to obtain a paid position. Recognize that one of the best aspects of landing an internship in your field of interest is that you experience the day-to-day existence of a person in that profession. This can be tremendously motivating... *or* it might turn you off to the profession entirely. (Obviously, either outcome is a valuable data point.) Again, make sure you have worked with the Career Center to design an effective resume before you strike out on your job search.

A few final words on your choice of a major: **Your major does not have to "equal" your career.** Let's say that your major is in history. Does this mean you will necessarily be an historian? Of course not! A background in history is also excellent preparation for journalism, law, government and a wide range of other fields. In much the same way, a computer science major might lead you into the field of graphic art or film editing.

If you've hit a wall in your major, sometimes you just have to change it. Lots of once-aspiring electrical engineers end up as perfectly happy architects or economists. —**L.M.**

I was a chronic major-changer. I started in electrical engineering, tried political science for a season and ended up studying Latin by my sophomore year. Finally, I realized what my problem was. There was no major program at my university that incorporated all the classes I loved, i.e., foreign languages, economics, political science and history. So I scheduled a meeting with the director of the college of arts and sciences and laid out my plan for an interdisciplinary bachelor degree program in "International Relations." The faculty and courses to support this interdisciplinary major had long existed, but nobody had put the pieces together. After slicing through some of the usual bureaucracy my new major was approved. From that day forward my undergrad experience took on a whole new meaning. I felt a great deal more invested in my degree program because I had spent the time and energy to define my own path. So if the course catalog gives you lemons, learn to make lemonade. —**J.P.**

My aim in this section is merely to get you thinking about how your major will influence and shape your future career – and to see if we can get your career in gear even *before* you leave college. Let's say you decide you want to be a lawyer and focus your efforts on speaking with attorneys in various areas of the law. But then, upon graduation, you decide you want to work for a high-flying business consulting firm and skip law school. Does this mean your forays into the legal field have been in vain? Nope. Your experience interacting with professionals and building contacts will serve you well in whatever you do. You will be able to distinguish yourself clearly from the hordes of unfocused interview virgins who are floundering around as they try to luck into a suitable career after college.

Chapter XIV

Snagging A Good Gig:
It's All About Persistence

Key Points

1. Choose a major, but recognize that it need not "equal" your future career.

2. Follow a stepwise plan to investigate careers.

Chapter XIV Notes

1. By the way, "undeclared" status may mean you get defaulted to a liberal arts classification. This is great if you ultimately decide to pursue a liberal arts degree. But delaying your switch to a new major could delay your graduation if you don't fulfill your requirements in time.

Grow up – or you'll just grow old. –**G.F.**

Chapter XV

Accepting Adulthood: You Can Run But You Can't Hide

A High-Yield Investment: Yourself

I want to leave you with some useful ideas for success in life out-side of the classroom – during your college years and beyond.

There are many important things we are not taught in school, among them:

(1) How to be a good husband or wife,

(2) How to raise kids, and

(3) How to manage money.

I won't presume to try to give you a plan to deal with these three daunting areas in the next few pages (especially since I have no idea about the first two things).

I only mention these conspicuous educational gaps to emphasize just how much critical knowledge society expects you to acquire on your own. Because of this, most successful people have done a lot of **self-education**. Come to think of it, you're self-educating right now.

Four Out Of Five Experts

Here is a fantastic goal you can set for yourself once a year: develop an area of expertise in an area outside of your college curriculum that interests you. This annual project is enjoyable, useful and goes a long way toward demystifying the credential-oriented learning process.

Let's say you take me up on this and decide to become a junior expert at something. How do people become "experts" anyway? And in a related question, how do people become "professors"? The paramount requirement is that they cultivate an avid interest in a given subject. Of course, the educational "system" also requires professors to engage in a lengthy roster of accredited undergraduate and graduate coursework. If their work is adequate, a series of degrees are conferred upon them, usually including a Ph.D. But on a basic level, they just read, study and write with great enthusiasm. Then they get to "profess" about what they have read and thought about.

While professors are to be revered for their hard work and their accomplishments, you should not tremble in intimidation at their knowledge. Remember, they too were once good students who at age 18 were themselves performing assignments much like the ones they are now assigning. Moreover, if we don't question our experts we are susceptible to being bamboozled.

So let's say you take an interest in the life and writings of Mark Twain, or in the history of aeronautics. Cultivate that interest. Read all you can. Seek out others with the same interest. Throw yourself into your hobby or interest in your free time and you will realize that there is no vast chasm between you and any degreed expert you encounter.

Root Beer And Bacon Bits? Fried Chicken And Yoo-Hoo? You Are What You Eat.

would be lying if I said I wanted you to read this book and just "take it or leave it." I really hope you take all or most of it to heart. Let's say I wanted to give you some advice about, say, your diet.

Some of you would be indignant. *"Oh no he didn't... Girl, he is not gonna tell me how to eat!"* Okay, okay – but hear me out for one second because I'm just trying to make myself useful.

Humans evolved from tree-bound primates into large-brained, high-IQ bipeds through a diet of natural, unprocessed foods. This occurred over hundreds of thousands of years. Can you imagine how those early primates would have developed had they instead eaten the fast food diets of today during those many millennia? How would we have evolved had our ancestors gorged on greasy burgers, super-sized soft drinks, buckets of fried chicken and bushels of French fries?[1] I'm imagining a creature called *"homo lard-assus triple-bypassus"* – an obese, largely immobile, walnut-brained, depressed, potato-like species with a mercifully brief life span.

Dude, use your head, feed your brain, and eat what got you here. Here are a few tips:

(1) Karmelkorn® is not a breakfast.

(2) Eat some lean protein with each meal – especially breakfast. Protein is nature's appetite suppressant without which you will feel hungry before your next meal. The idea is to eat at regular times, always including some protein, so that you avoid coming to the meal table when you are starving. When famished you typically eat more than your body can comfortably use.

(3) The system in the human body that regulates whether or not you are hungry or thirsty is highly inaccurate. Often you'll find that if you wait five minutes after you've eaten what may have seemed like a small portion – rather than going for a second helping – you're suddenly not hungry anymore.

"Homo lard-assus triple-bypassus"

"Tubby" the modern-day freshman.

(4)   In general, don't eat less than two hours before you go to bed. You burn the most fat before you sleep – *unless* you fill up the tank late at night.

(5)   Eat something green at least twice a day. (I mean like a vegetable, not a lime-flavored popsicle).

(6)   Incorporate salmon into your diet. Fish is the most potent brain-food you can eat. (Mercury content in larger fish that tend to accumulate toxins, such as tuna, is a legitimate concern so moderate your intake of these species.)

(7)   If a product includes *any* of the following on its list of ingredients, it has negligible nutritional value and you should **avoid** eating or drinking it:

• white flour

• refined sugar (especially soft drinks)

• "non-fat" products that contain a lot of sugar (these products deceive the public since this sugar is quickly transformed into fat)

• "hydrogenated" or "partially-hydrogenated" oils

• corn syrup (this cheap sweetener is in a ton of "healthy" things that are really crap – no matter what the label claims)

• any high-carbohydrate food that is not a vegetable or fruit (pastas and breads of all kinds) should be eaten sparingly (and no, I'm not telling you to follow Atkins – eat all the vegetables you can with the exception of potatos, which are extremely starchy and will put weight on you).

- anything dispensed from a vending machine except for bottled water.

- anything sold by any restaurant that furnishes toys to children as a regular part of its food service activities.

(8) If you do overindulge in Ben & Jerry's new "Karamel Sutra" flavor ("Soft Caramel Encircled by Chocolate & Caramel Ice Cream & Fudge Chips"), let a stairmaster become your confessional booth. Exercise is absolution for virtually all nutritional sins. It follows that if you can combine a decent diet with exercise you will become a Greek god – or at least not a chunky load of goo.

If, on the other hand, you are interested in being fat and tired, ignore all of this advice. Hey, nobody has a perfect diet, but just keep these ideas in mind and strive for incremental changes. Tiny improvements make a huge difference over time.[2] Trust in that knowledge. Give in to that belief. And stick with your plan even if you can't see the changes for a few weeks. Somebody else may actually notice before you do.

Fun With Sugar

Don't believe sugar is poison? Here's a cool experiment. Hold one of your arms straight out, horizontally and to the side. Have a buddy hold your arm in place with his hand as you try your best to push your arm above shoulder level. You should be able to apply good upward pressure against your friend's hand as he holds your arm down.

Next, take a pack of white sugar and empty the contents under your tongue. Wait about a minute as the sugar dissolves in your mouth and is released sub-lingually into your bloodstream. Now try pressing your arm up against the resistance of your friend's hand again. Most likely you will find that your strength has been noticeably diminished as the Satanic white sugar sends your energy crashing downward. Neat, huh? But should you be doing this to yourself several times a day when what you need from your body is peak physical and mental efficiency?

Unfortunately, artificial and chemical sweeteners all have their own side effects, though a product like Splenda® is worlds better than sugar. But the best product out there is all-natural–and actually *good* for you! It's called Stevia and it is made from an herb discovered centuries ago in Central America. Stevia is actually sweeter than sugar, non-caloric and can be purchased at vitamin and grocery stores in convenient packets–just like the poisonous stuff.

Why haven't more people heard about pure, healthy, delicious, natural, useful Stevia? Because, until recently, manufacturers of sugar, chemical sweeteners and other financially interested industries have been successful in keeping it out of stores. Sad but true.

Are You Alive?

I f you are not exercising regularly, you are hardly alive. Just barely chugging along, if you will. Fundamentally, your body was designed to be exercised. Indeed, its complex pumping and suctioning machinery *needs* physical exertion to properly pass blood, lymph and other fluids throughout your body. Without exercise, your blood does not receive sufficient amounts of cleansing, nourishing oxygen. If you remain sedentary your body cannot properly flush out the toxins that build up in your system. Toxins make you tired and more prone to illness.

A half-hour of daily exercise is a good goal to work toward. Frankly, it doesn't matter how you get there. Whether you choose to walk briskly for twenty minutes each day and slowly work your way up, or if you prefer to put aerobics or weight training into your exercise mix, just be consistent.[3] Eventually, you will want to incorporate some resistance exercise, which studies show is a veritable fountain of youth–even for people in their 90's.

Many successful people honor themselves with at least a small amount of strenuous physical activity each day. Model what they do and make exercise a high priority. Check out **www.kickasscam-pus.com** for effective and efficient exercise strategies.

Safer Sex

Is anyone so sexually desirable that you would literally give your life to have sex with them once? If the answer is yes, and you have a date with that person, don't worry about safe sex.

Otherwise, insist on condom use if you plan to have sex. Unfortunately, you need to be concerned about more than HIV/AIDS. As unromantic as it sounds you also need to find a graceful way to check your partner for any unusual lesions or skin conditions "down there." Anything unusual may indicate that they are contagious with any number of other painful, unpleasant and permanent diseases. Condoms are helpful in this situation but not entirely effective (against either disease *or* pregnancy[4]).

Alas, even careful visual examination guarantees nothing, and under no circumstances should you avoid condom use (unless you're placing an order for a baby and everyone's been thoroughly tested).

Times have changed. If you don't feel comfortable enough to be able to discuss these issues then maybe you shouldn't be having sex with that person. Otherwise, you may find yourself with a reminder of your old flame as indelible as a tattoo (on your privates, unfortunately) long after the relationship may have ended.

Get yourself routinely tested for sexually transmitted diseases (STDs) at the campus medical center if you are sexually active. You can learn everything you ever wanted to know about sex (but were afraid to ask) if you pay them a visit. While there's no such thing as 100% safe sex that's what you're shooting for.

The Only Reason You Need To Avoid Drugs

H ere it is: Drugs increase your likelihood of passing on genetic defects to your children.

If you aren't planning on having children, then all you have to worry about is the risk of a lengthy and embarrassing prison term during which you could be brutalized or even murdered.

The Only Reason You Need To Avoid Cigarettes

C igarette companies have long relied on public ignorance with regard to health issues to turn a profit. The most vulnerable are the young and the poor. If you think these companies have revised their moral stance due to recent lawsuits in the U.S., well they haven't. They have simply redoubled their efforts to sell their products in Asia and Latin America. Read all about it – it's in their reassuring annual reports to shareholders.

These people don't care about you. They just want to addict you to their worthless (yet paradoxically expensive) products. So stop making them rich and helping them spread their deadly addiction to other people – in countries where the dangers of smoking are not as well understood.

If you smoke, go to your college health center and pick up a nicotine cessation kit so you can quit. If you don't smoke, there's no upside to starting – unless you want to look and feel considerably older. Sure, a lot of sexy young stars smoke. They also get daily facials, massage and thousands of dollars of plastic surgery before they turn 30[5].

For Chrissakes, Is This Guy Also Going To Tell Me I Can't Drink?

N ot exactly. I think it's pretty reasonable and realistic to ask you to avoid smoking and drugs. But for a number of reasons, logical or not, alcohol consumption continues to enjoy enormous so-cial acceptance. And, of course, many people have learned to use alcohol responsibly.

In America and in most of the world we have laws that set age limits for voting, joining the military, being married and, yes, drinking. You may find it inconsistent and silly that you can be sent to die in a war before you can legally drink a beer. If, however, you intend to drink as a minor there may be legal and other consequences. You are old enough to make that decision (paradoxical, isn't it?) so I won't lecture you. Instead, let's look at this from a practical perspective.

My major problem with drinking *at any age* is when a person doesn't know how to do it properly. For starters, they get really drunk – so drunk they think they can sing. They think they can drive. They think they can fly.

The worst thing about being a Resident Assistant in the dorm was dealing with all the drunk kids who couldn't hold their liquor. There were a couple of real jerks who lived down the hall from me. They would get blasted and yell at the top of their lungs when everyone else was trying to sleep. One night I awoke to the strange sound of liquid spattering outside my room. When I opened my door I couldn't believe my eyes. One of these morons was holding his Johnson with both hands and urinating on my door. He looked up at me, tottering around like a bowling pin–apparently not realizing that he was missing the toilet by about 22 feet. I was pretty groggy but the next thing I knew I had this guy on the ground, wringing his neck with both hands. Fortunately, the ruckus woke up the whole place (I must have been screaming in his face as I tried to choke the life out of him) and I was thus prevented by

my fellow RA's from acquiring a criminal record.[6]—**M.R.**

If I were King of the World I would require college students to sit through a class on how to drink responsibly. It would be taught by a stocky, street-smart bartender named Sal (not some tumbler-flipping pretty boy). Sal would tell you how to order, what to drink, what not to drink, and what kind of beverages don't mix well in the same stomach. For example, any good barkeep will tell you that if you chug a shot of 151-proof rum, a shot of Apple schnapps, and a Long Island Ice Tea one right after the other your stomach will explode, spattering the room with your entrails. It's very much like what they say happens when a seagull eats an Alka-Seltzer® tablet.

My parents' advice on drinking served me well. They knew I was going to do it so rather than trying to stop me they just asked me to follow three rules (which seem especially important for young women):

1. Never drink the "trashcan punch," since you have no idea what's in it.

2. Never let somebody at a party mix a drink for you.

3. Always have a glass of water between drinks.

I didn't always follow these rules to a tee, but I did so enough to stay out of trouble. Now you have to be even more careful with the "date rape" drugs out there. I won't even accept an open beer from somebody I don't know. —**K.V.**

Make a pact never to leave your girlfriends stranded at parties. You'll find it's hard to live up to this "pact" when alcohol and cute guys are involved, but they'll thank you in the morning. And if they don't they're probably slutty anyway. (Just kidding... but not really because there's always one or two horndogs in every group.) —E.Y.

The real trouble with drinking while you are in college, even in "moderation," is that each time you raise a glass you risk lowering a grade. If you have even a *little* too much alcohol you lose productive study time, possibly losing the next day to a hangover. When you finally get down to studying your body may be begging you for a nap. In this situation you are denying yourself the long-term pleasure of doing well in school in exchange for the short-term pleasure of throwing up.

Then there's the problem of habit-forming consumption of alcohol. *Ay ay ay.* Are you sure you want to train yourself to associate drinking with "fun" and "the good life"?

When I look back on my undergrad years, I recall that they were a very fluid portion of my life—by that I mean, I drank a lot of fluids, mainly beer. As a result, the first time I tried going to college I basically failed out. The second time, I switched to coffee, got my degree, and continued drinking coffee straight through business school. I still drink too much coffee. Makes me a little jumpy but it's better than stumbling in to work drunk. —A.R.

Funny thing about drinking booze...it's an "adult" activity that starts to seem less adult the older you get. Bottom line, keep a short leash on any drinking you choose to do, okay? Things can really get ugly–read on.

Baby You Can't Drive My Car

As you probably know, the law cuts you no slack if you drink and maim. If you hurt somebody on the road, you are toast–in addition to having a horrible burden on your conscience for the rest of your life.

Next time you visit a hospital ask a nurse to show you some patients in the intensive care unit who are recovering (or not recovering) from car crashes. And try not to pass out when you see their mangled bodies. Sometimes everybody in the house is there because of a drunk driver.

If you're ever in a situation where you happen to be the last person on earth, hook a funnel on to a Margarita machine and fire up the Chevy. But in the meantime, you have no right to roll the dice with anybody else's life.

Here's my rule. It's really easy to remember:

"Don't Drink A Drop If You Plan To Drive."

It's not that radical a concept if you think about it. Sweden, for example, has a zero-tolerance law when it comes to drinking. The Swedes can drink with the best of them, but the law over there is that if you have *any* alcohol in your system whatsoever, and you get caught behind the wheel, you can kiss your license goodbye...*forever*. I may sound like a hardass but I actually think they have the right idea.

You wouldn't let it slide if somebody shot a gun just a tiny bit recklessly around you or your family, would you? Maybe a beer or two won't make you "drunk" but it will increase–at least slightly–the possibility that your car becomes a deadly weapon while you drive. **Any time you even slightly increase the chance of killing, maiming or burning somebody alive–that's significant.**[7]

Informally Speaking

Many colleges and independent organizations periodically offer short or "informal" classes. These classes usually last a couple of nights, and feature instruction by local professionals. The wide variety of classes I have seen include:

Wok Cooking
Money Management
Relaxation Techniques
Build Your Own Website
How to Write & Sell Nonfiction
Improving Your Relationships
Public Speaking for Scaredy Cats
Learn Microsoft Excel
Improve Your Memory
How to Run a Small Business
Learn to Play Golf
Stand-Up Comedy Workshop
Camping and Hiking Expedition

For a small enrollment fee, you can participate in an enriching learning experience, often with members of your faculty and the local community. This is an excellent way to supplement your college education. There are also an endless variety of on-line seminars available at www.learningannex.com.

Granted, some of the offerings you'll see are pretty, um, shall we say, "offbeat" (*e.g.*, "Establish a Psychic Connection with Your Pet" and "Learn to Strip for Your Lover"), but don't let that turn you off (or on). There are always plenty of more mainstream courses to choose from.

Years ago – long before I had two dimes to rub together – I took a course called "Real Estate for Beginners." That six-hour class helped prepare me to make some simple investments that now produce a significant portion of my annual income. I'm sure you've heard that good luck happens when "preparation meets opportunity." It's up to you to use your time productively so that you are always in the process of preparing yourself for opportunities you will encounter in the future.

Drive Your Library

A terrific way to get the latest books and newspapers in down-loadable format, at a deep discount, is through www.audible. com. You will be blown away by the selection.

You can process a ton of information while driving in your car. If you are ever faced with a lengthy trip, especially cross-country, make the most of it. Don't just grab your music – grab your books as well.

Turbo-Linguistics

If you've ever wanted to learn a foreign language quickly, before you go on some travel abroad – this is your lucky day. In just a few 30-minute lessons on CD the Pimsleur language series can teach you how to have basic conversations in virtually every major language, from Spanish to Polish to Turkish to Thai. I've tried many language systems but this one really does what it promises in the amount of time it claims. *Ching ching, kap! Pome pood Thai dai dee maak maak, kap!* (It's true! I can speak great Thai!)

By the way, if you plan to travel to another country and you don't speak the language you should pick up a pocket two-way diction-ary. This allows you, for example, to look for the word "pharmacy" in English and find the Chinese character right next to it, and vice-versa. Foreigners (except, of course, for the French) are usually quite flattered when you try to learn a few words of their language and they will treat you 53% better when you do.

Think Positive ... Cash Flow

Proper budgeting is crucial to your quality of life in college and beyond. Again, many members of your freshman class will buy the academic farm due to financial pressure. Most students have a tendency to overspend when they first arrive at college, especially if they haven't quite "learned the value of money" as Mom or Dad might put it.

Organizing your finances is one of life's most basic priorities. If you don't control your money it will control *you*. And it is a harsh and merciless sumbitch that will eat your lunch and put you in chains for as long as you let it. Money can end friendships. Money can destroy families. Money can even *kill* with the stress it causes.

But when your money is working for you, and you tame your finances, that's a different story altogether. Money can be freedom. Money can provide education. Money can do beautiful things.

Sure, we've all heard the old saying: "Money can't buy happiness." But in the words of Bob Hope: "Happiness can't buy money."

You need a basic money plan for now, and you need to commit to learning about money as time marches on. Having well-defined financial goals is an important part of money management. A recent study showed that, among people with the same incomes, those who had a financial plan saved at least twice as much as those who did not. I guarantee that if you get educated about money you will make – and keep – much more of it.

Here are my ten strategies to keep you afloat financially, academically and emotionally:

(1) To recap, do everything you can to secure enough financial aid loans and/or grants to avoid a job to the extent possible. Really, try to max out. School work, not another job or extracurricular activities, is your number one priority. Some students can't resist getting a job so they can pick up a little extra spending money. But they may be jeopardizing their ability to make a good salary after they graduate, when it really counts. Just get into the best school you can and the money will come.

(2) Write out a simple, realistic budget and stick to it. Nothing fancy. Goes a little something like this...

A. Itemize your annual sources of income (including the summers):

Financial aid
Parental support
Other income

Add these together, dividing by 12 to come up with what you have to work with on a monthly basis.

B. Itemize your estimated annual expenses (again, let's include summers):

Tuition and other school fees
Books & Supplies
Housing
Groceries
Transportation
Clothes
Scheduled bill payments (utilities, etc.)
Entertainment (eating out, movies, etc.)

Add these together, extrapolating a monthly estimate of your expenses.

In the best of all possible worlds, your expenses would be at least $100 dollars less than the sum of your total income. Set this money aside for medical, dental, automobile and other emergencies. Ideally, you are also a beneficiary of your parents' medical insurance (if not, socking a little cash away is even more important).

(3) **Bank on it:** If you don't have one already, open a checking account. (Look for a national bank that caters to students for maximum convenience and minimum fees.) Next, open a savings account. If you have set a savings goal for the year and you can meet it early (due to a windfall, or for whatever reason), go for it. If you can earmark $100 dollars a month for savings, as I suggest above, that would mean you will accumulate $1,200 dollars by year's end. Consider this money untouchable. By the end of college you will have, with interest, nearly $5,000 dollars in the bank. Of course, if you have no savings plan or budget and simply let the chips fall where they may, you may have *zero* in the bank–along with the soul-crushing anxiety of being broke. (Beware: ATM cards issued to you by your bank can be overdraft-magnets. Keep track of every transaction in your checkbook or you can easily get slapped with overdraft charges of around $30 dollars per check–more if the bank refuses to honor the check and you *also* get slapped with similar returned check fees by the party to whom you wrote the check. So they basically get you coming and going. We all go through this and it really sucks –but it's just one of those life-lessons people seem to need to learn the hard way.)

(4) **Even if you don't save one red cent, for God's sake don't go into credit card debt.** Credit card debt is the number one financial problem affecting college students today. Those companies camped out in front of the book store giving away free tee-shirts are more than happy to offer you credit. They know that the average monthly credit card balance for a college student is in the neighborhood of $600 dollars. Credit cards foster the illusion that you are getting something for nothing. It's a great little scam. Credit cards promise "low monthly payments" of twenty to thirty dollars. These bloodsuckers love

it if you pay low monthly payments because that means you'll never pay off the balance. Your interest charge is usually between 18 and 21% a year! If you only send in the minimum monthly payment, you will merely be paying the interest for the rest of your life. The trouble is, most college students can't afford to pay more than the minimum payment. Get the picture? Now do you see why they're lining up to offer you credit? They figure they can enslave you in debt for at least four years if not much, much longer.

(5) Still not convinced that credit cards are the Devil? Think about this: If you buy a pair of sneakers on credit for around $100 dollars, and you are unable to pay off your balance for months or years, you will pay for those shoes several times over in interest charges. Next time you buy something on credit, multiply the cost by two, three, or four so you can get a better idea of what you're getting into.

(6) It is important to develop a good credit rating. And you can start now by paying your phone and utility bills on time, for example. Once you get out into the work force a bank will offer you a low-interest credit card, which will also help. Even then, use your credit card (you should only have one) only in case of absolute emergencies, and pay off the entire balance before you are charged any interest.

(7) If you already find yourself in serious credit card trouble, the United Way offers free consumer credit counseling. They can enroll you in money management seminars and deal directly with your creditors to give you some financial breathing room. Sometimes we have to learn things the hard way – just so long as you remember the lesson.

(8) If possible and practical, shop at Costco® stores. There are other membership-based discount grocery stores that offer products in bulk at cut-rate prices but Costco really rocks. They have great customer service, all kinds of name-brand products and they treat their employees exceptionally well. The membership fee pays for itself on your first visit. You can save a lot of money investing a big tub of detergent, for example, instead of buying little boxes at the local convenience store. Same goes for toilet paper, shampoo, and other household items. But there's no need to buy the place out. You don't want to save yourself into bankruptcy. Besides, you can always come back after you polish off that first 112-pack of Charmin.

(9) Look into an economical dormitory meal plan. They are often available to you even if you don't live in a dorm, or in the particular dorm where you wish to eat. Otherwise, whenever possible, cook for yourself and prepare your own beverages and snacks. The amount of money you will save by avoiding fast food and vending machines is astounding, not to speak of the health benefits. If you don't know anything about cooking, invest in an informal class and learn a skill that will benefit you for life. You'll beat yourself with a rolling pin for not having done it sooner.

(10) Read "The Richest Man in Babylon" by George S. Clason. This slim little book, usually available at the library, will give you invaluable insight into money matters and will guide your thinking for a lifetime. Please read it.

Alternatives To Country Music?

I've alluded to the importance of surrounding yourself with positive people who respect your ambition to perform well. This is one way to create a healthy, upbeat environment for achieving your goals. More fundamentally, I'm also talking about maintaining a positive mental attitude by controlling your intake of information.

In many ways, your immediate mental state, your happiness and even your health is determined by the information to which you are exposed. (It is reported, for example, that two-thirds of medical students acquire the symptoms of the particular disease they happen to be studying!) Your mood, and its effects on your mind and body, happen minute to minute.

I recently picked up a novel that went in a direction I hadn't anticipated – it began exploring some pretty horrific examples of prison abuse. I made the decision that I didn't need another six or eight hours of immersion in that world so I simply put it down. Was that book interesting? Sure, in a morbid sort of way. But there are certain things you can't unread, or unhear, or unsee. Why give such disturbing or negative images real estate in your mind? We all have plenty of that mental baggage as it is.

The obvious exception is when tragic information or images are necessary to our education, and to our understanding of history or current events. But do you have to watch the videos of hostages being brutally murdered to understand current international conflicts? I didn't and I don't plan to.

One way to maximize your chances of experiencing a positive, happy outlook is to avoid needlessly injecting your reality with toxic material that digs you into an emotional hole. Look, I've got nothing against going to a movie to watch a poignant, heartbreaking story, or with experiencing those raw and gritty aspects of life that are not all sweetness and light.

I only want you to be aware that what (and who) you surround yourself with directly impacts your state of being. Maybe the next time you reach for that sad country song or that gratuitously violent rap track, ask yourself if you really want your mental state to be altered in the way it will be when the music starts. Is that behavior really making you "happy," or are putting yourself in a less desirable place? It's different for everybody.

The strange thing about happiness is that it tends to happen when we aren't even paying attention. We may not even fully realize we're happy until later. Happiness can be a delicate sensation so we need to be open and receptive when it knocks at our door. And without extended periods of happiness, "success" is meaningless, and our goals will never be fulfilled in any meaningful sense. So it's up to you to protect your happiness by taking in as much positive information as possible. You are a product of your environment – an environment that you can increasingly control as your life goes on.

Let the Goth kids have their fun with black clothes and annihilating sadness. You dwell on the things that are going to make you more successful.

Tit For Tats

When we're young a lot of us go through a prolonged "look at me" phase. That might involve unusual fashions that make us feel extremely silly a decade later. It is my profound hope that laser technology will improve in the next five years to permit the easy removal of the untold millions of bad tattoos Gen X, Y and now Z have applied to their bodies. There may come a day when you'll wish you had the option of not having that Chinese character for "stallion" on your neck (or whatever).

We may violently disagree on this but I'm all about preserving your options. You may think I'm speaking to you from a soulless, sold-out place but the reality *is you will be wearing a "uniform" of some kind for the rest of your life.* And facial scarification and a nose-bone probably won't be part of it (unless, in fairness, you work at a funky graphic arts firm or ad agency, but those kinds of professional environments are uncommon). Please think long and hard about presenting yourself in any kind of "look at me" matter. This goes quadruply for any permanent changes to your body.

I'm all about freedom of expression but adults do not indulge this freedom to the detriment of other freedoms – like the freedom to make a living. (If you want to flame me on this, my email appears at the end.)

We all wear a "uniform" of some kind.

When I was an undergraduate physics student I had long hair and looked every bit the stoner. When I would walk down the street the homeless hustlers would regularly approach me to talk shop. Funny thing is, at this time in my life, I was taking 20+ hours per semester, I had a 4.0 G.P.A., and I had quit drinking, smoking and dating. I was

singularly focused on learning math and physics. On the weekends, I would give my college ID card to the Physics Department so that I could check out a key to the physics lab. One Saturday, I decided to take myself to see the big football game as a special treat. But since I didn't have my ID the security guard would not let me, the "hippie," past the gate. Just after me in the line was a clean-cut "frat boy." He was three sheets to the wind with his flask of rum in his back pocket. He slurred his words in explaining that he had forgotten his ID card. Nevertheless, the guard let him in to the game, while I sat out and listened to the crowd roar as the home team pummeled the visitors. (Oh, did I mention it was my birthday?) Anyway, I guess the moral of the story is that sometimes looks really matter. We don't always want to believe it but that's the harsh truth. —**N.M.**

Look, it's just like my Mom used to tell me, *"Te tratan como te ven"* (they'll treat you with as much respect as you command by your appearance).

Golf, Tennis Or Skiing Anyone?

There will be many times in your life as a professional when you will be happy you learned a sport that enjoys popularity in the corporate world. If you can participate in this kind of activity you increase your opportunities to build good relationships in the workplace and to "court" clients.

Don't worry if you've never participated in these activities. A beginner's class and, ideally, some private instruction will give you a terrific jump start. Learning one of these sports is like a lifetime gift you give to yourself.

Once, Twice, Three Times A Student

This last thing may sound a little weird at first, so strap in. Here's a useful perspective on successfully living with yourself as you strive to achieve your goals. I ask students to think of themselves as three separate people:

1. The person they were in the past.

2. The person they are in the present.

3. The person they will be in the future.

Have you ever heard that really inane expression, "Be your own best friend"? Strangely enough, this is a pretty good policy. You should always seek to be good to yourself. More precisely, you should be good to your three selves. What does this mean?

1. **Being good to your "past self" means ...** forgiving yourself for your failures: your bad tests, your dumb comments, your failed relationships, your embarrassing episodes, your perceived shortcomings, and anything else that may be bothering you about your past. You must learn to clear away the negative residue that may be gumming up your mind. Take action and confront these thoughts. Talk them out with a friend, a parent or a counselor. Do not merely sweep a painful thought under the carpet or endlessly punish yourself. You can always go back and make amends to heal a relationship. There is great strength in the knowledge that you can always course-correct and perform better. I've given you a lot of advice in this book. Maybe you haven't been following it. Maybe you won't follow it all and wish you had. You only have yourself to answer to. Be forgiving but also make a serious and solemn commitment to yourself to do better. (And when it comes to failing because you tried something new or you pursued your passion, do not be afraid to fail! Failure of this kind is absolutely necessary to success!)

2. **Being good to your "present self" means...** taking control of your emotions and state of mind so that you can think lucidly and make good decisions *in the moment.* Take a second to assess your mood and stress level before addressing difficult problems. (If you're losing it, take deep breaths, exhaling for twice as long as you inhale.) Don't allow yourself to be pressured, hurried or coerced by time, circumstances or people.

3. **Being good to your "future self" means...** taking care of things *now.* Don't allow your workspace or your living area to become messy. Don't make rash financial choices (like using a credit card for frivolous expenses). Don't make unreasonable study plans (heaving all-nighters) that will cause you suffering and hardship in the future. Don't go out and party when you know damn well you'll regret it. Have some compassion for yourself–for the poor, tired, guilty person you will be if you do not act responsibly.

Wrap It Up, G

These are the basics of a winning academic philosophy. Use these strategies and you will gain a whole new appreciation of your potential. College is a lot more fun when you decide to succeed, and follow a plan to do so. ***Always remember that focus on the future will give you motivation in the present.*** If you ever feel your intellectual engine begin to stall, sharpen your focus. See and touch and taste your success in your mind and it will happen.

In the meantime, always do a little more than other people expect of you and you'll be all right.

* * *

I hope you enjoyed this conversation as much as I did. Sometimes, certain words echo in your mind long after you hear or read them. I hope some of the words you picked up here serve you both now and in years to come.

I would welcome hearing about your success in college and beyond. Feel free to email me at **gunnar@kickassincollege.com**.

Now go kick ass!

Chapter XV

Accepting Adulthood: You Can Run But You Can't Hide

Key Points

1. Read this final chapter twice. It's all important. And good luck out there!

Chapter XV Notes

1. Fast food intake by American children has increased five-fold since 1970. For God's sake, see Morgan Spurlock's hilarious but chilling documentary, "Super-Size Me." It may save your life.

2. You can't accomplish any fitness goal all at once. Fast weight loss, for example, is simply against nature. We all know that. Recall that correctly engineered goals are "Specific" and "Time-bound." Set a goal in pounds but break it into the specific number of ounces you need to lose per day. (This helps you recognize the connection between small, manageable differences in the quality and amounts of the food you eat.) If you are pursuing a weight or fitness goal, you should also post, along with your written goals, an inspirational photo of a person whose body you are seeking to emulate. Needless to say, this kind of image placed where you can see it every day will assist you in your visualization. Study it with intensity a couple of times a day.

3. Folks with physical limitations are by no means exempt. You and your doctor or physical therapist can dream up dozens of workouts even if you don't have full mobility.

4. Always combine condom use with birth-control pills and spermicide for maximum protection against pregnancy. You may wish to consult with the health center regarding the so-called "morning-after pill" if you experience condom breakage or other contraceptive failure. If you or your sexual partner become pregnant, and you wish to consider other options besides taking the pregnancy to term as permitted by law, consult your health center or local hospital *immediately*.

5. And as for the strategy of smoking as a weight-loss method, you're better off trying amputation. You have a far greater chance of surviving the loss of a limb or two than you do lung cancer, or any of the dozens of other often fatal diseases caused or exacerbated by sucking on those little death sticks.

6. By the way, if a friend ever calls you to help bail him out of jail you have to do it. Count on it taking all night.

7. The same dangers arise when using phones and PDA's behind the wheel. Just momentary inattention behind the wheel–it doesn't take much– can destroy lives.

Join the

KICK ASS IN COLLEGE
Community

We invite you to visit **www.kickasscampus.com** for more academic and life advice, a Q & A forum, discounts on *Kick Ass in College*™ products and school gear, and other great stuff for success-minded students.

To collect your **FREE gift worth $49.95** send an email to:

gift@kickassincollege.com.

About The Artists

Alan Aldridge, Logo Concept

Alan Aldridge's world-renowned graphic images have adorned record albums for the Beatles, Elton John and Tears for Fears. His art continues to exert a deep influence on our culture through his popular illustrations for the House of Blues as well as his prolific book jacket and logo designs. Alan now makes his home in Los Angeles.

www.alanaldridge.com

Scott Reed, Cover Design and Illustrations

After graduating from the Art Institute of Pittsburgh, Scott Reed began a career in graphic design and commercial art, producing illustrations and designs for Disney, Wal-Mart, Marvel Comics, United Way, Target, Remax, Home Depot and Paramount Pictures. Scott brings 15 years of graphic design experience to his full service studio, Web's Best Designs. Combining traditional illustration with cutting-edge computer graphics and web development, Scott provides unique, creative solutions to a wide variety of businesses. An award-winning cartoonist and designer and one of the pioneers of digital comics on the web, Scott's prolific and versatile work has been described as "old school" with a contemporary flair, and praised by USA Today and SciFi Channel as "stylish" and "cool."

www.websbestdesigns.com
www.websbestcomics.com

Send Us Your Tips
and Enter the Gigantor

KICK ASS IN COLLEGE
Raffle!

Got a kick-ass study tip or some great advice for academic or life success? Please email us at **publisher@kickassmedia.com**, and include your name (unless you prefer to be anonymous). Any submission makes you eligible for the "Gigantor *Kick Ass in College*™ Raffle" with prizes to include a palmOne® handheld Personal Digital Assistant and other great awards. Selected entries will also receive special mention in the next edition of *Kick Ass in College*. Send in your tips today!

(All entries become property of KickAssMedia.)

KICK ASS IN COLLEGE

(Bulk Discounts Available)

To order please visit **www.kickassmedia.com**
or call us toll-free at 1-877-MY COOL BOOK
or Fax the order form below to: 1-877-692-7441
or Mail this order form to the address below:

KickAssMedia
12358 Coit Road, PMB#317
Dallas, TX 75251-2308

- -

Please rush me ____ copies of *Kick Ass in College* @ $16.95 U.S.

= $ _____

Please rush me ____ copies of *Kick Ass in College* on Audio CD @ $24.95 U.S.

= $ _____

Please rush me my **FREE** gift worth $49.95 U.S. to this email: _____

= $49.95 ***FREE!***

(no shipping fee)

Postage & Handling ____ items @ $5.00 U.S./$10.00 International for first item
($2.00 per each add'l item)
for **RUSH** delivery ____ items @ $15.00 U.S./$30.00 International for first item
($5.00 per each add'l item)

= $ _____

Subtotal of merchandise = $ _____

Texas Residents: Add 8.25% tax to your order
(simply multiply SUBTOTAL x 1.0825)

= $ _____

TOTAL = $ _____

Privacy notice: we will not share your information with any party.

Ship to (Name): _____

Address: _____

City: _____ State/Province: _____

Country: _____ Zip/P.C.: _____

Phone: _____ Fax: _____ Email: _____

Method of Payment:

☐ Check – Please make payable to KAM and mail to the address shown above.
Charge to: ☐ Mastercard ☐ Visa ☐ American Express ☐ Discover

Name on Card: _____

Card Number: _____ Expiration: _____

Notes

Notes